Twelve Step Plan to Becoming an Actor in L.A.

Twelve Step Plan to Becoming an Actor in L.A.

From Your Town to Tinseltown

A definitive guide to "making it" in the world's toughest city for actors

Dawn Lerman & Dori Keller

iUniverse Star
New York Lincoln Shanghai

Twelve Step Plan to Becoming an Actor in L.A.
From Your Town to Tinseltown

iUniverse Star
an iUniverse, Inc. imprint

iUniverse books may be ordered through booksellers or by contacting:

iUniverse
2021 Pine Lake Road, Suite 100
Lincoln, NE 68512
www.iuniverse.com
1-800-Authors (1-800-288-4677)

This book solely represents the views of the authors, the following information in this book does not guarantee employment.

ISBN: 0-595-29793-5

Printed in the United States of America

To my children, Dylan and Sofia, who show me the true meaning of life's journey everyday.

CONTENTS

PREFACE

DAWN LERMAN

How are you getting to Los Angeles? Where are you going to live? What are you going to do when you get there? And what are your plans for getting it!! Whatever it is. These questions and many more like it were part of our experiences as young people who believed we were artists and wanted desperately to carve out our niche, our point of view, and ultimately our success in the entertainment industry.

I was not alone. Fourteen years ago, when I arrived in LA, there were approximately forty thousand actors in the Screen Actors Guild. I was naive and not up on the who's who and what's what in the business. However, I had passion and promise. This, and three hundred dollars, is what brought me to Hollywood.

Today the number of actors in the Screen Actors Guild is closer to seventy three thousand and the odds of succeeding are even more daunting today than they were then. I have worked hard over the years to sustain my initial excitement through success and rejection.

Growing up in New York City, I thought I had pretty much done it all. However, my arrival in LA threw me for a loop. Hollywood was anything but kind and glamorous, and its language, schmooze, was foreign to my ears and my way of thinking. Being a dreamer, I felt like a character out of a Jack Kerouac novel. I was adventurous and free-spirited and thought that nothing could touch me. I had absolutely everything I needed for my journey: my army green 8th street thrift store knapsack, my jeans, T-shirt, and high-top Keds. I also had my pictures, resumes, training, and the blessings of the celebrities I met while dancing my nights away at Studio 54. Through my nightclub escapades, I collected a pile of matchbook numbers, all with invitations to crash if I ever made it to LA. Friends and relatives berated me for being a Pollyanna, but I didn't care. I interpreted this as their jealousy because I had a dream and they didn't. I knew they couldn't imagine what it felt like to have a dream as strong as I did. I lived by the words of Tennessee Williams: "I don't want realism I want magic." Little did I know that there are serious repercussions to ignoring reality.

Through my experiences, I've learned many lessons. One is that reality is not a bad thing. As a matter of fact, it is necessary. I also learned that success is defined in many ways. It is a goal, not a way of life. By society's terms, I can be considered successful: I am an accomplished producer, writer, and drama therapist. How I define success now is very different. For me, success is giving—working with people and sharing my experiences and guiding them on their quest. This is my journey, a journey that is different for everyone. But what I do know, to be successful, you must have a dream. But a dream alone is dangerous. To achieve a dream, you need a plan, a plan that consists of concrete steps.

My partner Dori Keller and I often argue over life, how we view the entertainment business, and what success means. But we are definitely in accord on the fact that if you don't want to be devoured by the entertainment industry, you need a plan. We want to share our stories and experiences with other young actors to help them avoid some of the mistakes we made. We believe our experiences as well as the experiences from other actors—successful as well as struggling—will help you improve your chances of success in LA. This is why we have developed the Twelve Step Plan.

DORI KELLER

People sometimes ask why or even how I was able to leave acting after a fifteen year career. I left because I no longer found the joy in expressing who I was through that artistic choice. More was revealed through other means such as teaching, directing and producing—areas where I felt I had more creative control over the artistic process. Since that time, I have learned that a career moves from point to point. Where I am now is a stepping-stone that will lead me to the next step. By connecting the dots, I learned where I was, where I'd gone, and where and who I am now.

In the twenty years I've worked in the entertainment industry as actor, producer, development executive, and casting director, I have seen and heard many stories of success as well as heartbreak. Why is that? Why some actors and not others? Some of the answers to these questions are tangible; others, ephemeral. But for an overview of a career, one of the things I have learned is that it has little to do with how much talent an actor has.

This is an explosive statement, I understand. And yes, talent is important, but having the most talent is not what always gets you the job. According to Elia Kazan, one of the founders of the Actors Studio and director of a *Streetcar Named Desire* and *On the Waterfront,* "It's 90% attitude and perseverance, and 10% talent." It's how the actor feels about himself and his abilities that determine his career. An actor with a modicum of ability but with an abundance of self-belief succeeds. This is one of the cornerstones of my belief about life and a life in acting. It is also the motivation for writing this book that outlines the Twelve Step Plan to Becoming an Actor in LA. Before beginning the first of the Twelve Steps, you have to know this is your dream.

If you don't have to be an actor, DON'T! But if you do feel this is your calling, then create your journey with enthusiasm, a strong sense of self, and use this book as your road map.

ACKNOWLEDGMENTS

To Our Parents—Phyllis and Al Lerman, and Bob Keller.

Our friends—Shelly Desai, Robert Zuckerman, Frank Erowod, Harrison Young, April and Billy Jayne, April Haney, Ram Bergman, Silvia Beltrami, Jeremy Goldscheider, Eric Moses, Mishelle and Leon Owens, John Edwards, Arnie Weiss, Ron Hoiseck, Gabrielle Nash, Stephan Morrow, Maria, and all the other people who supported us and helped encourage us to write this book.

I'd also like to give special thanks to my editor and husband Todd Vaccaro for the preparation of this book.

And a special, special, thanks and gratitude to my co-editor and researcher Phyllis Carpenter for her hundreds of hours of hard work and dedication.

P.S.—Thank you Todd, for all the love, support, kindness, and peanut and jelly sandwiches.

INTRODUCTION

Has acting always been your dream? Have you ever stood in front of the bathroom mirror pretending you were accepting the Academy Award? Do you believe you are one of the chosen people? Do you go to the movies and plays and wonder how some actors have achieved such success and notoriety? You no longer have to wonder. You just need a plan—a road map on this journey called acting.

You can succeed with the proper focus, determination, and knowledge. *Twelve Step Plan To Becoming An Actor In LA* gives you the concrete steps, complemented by exercises, worksheets, quotes, interviews, and journal pages. We will ask you to constantly assess and reassess your goals, as well as take a daily, weekly, and monthly inventory of your progress. Becoming a professional actor is an interactive art. You need to think of it as a game, where you are competing not only against yourself, but also against the entertainment community.

Acting is instinctual. It is impulsive. Therefore, it is only natural that the decision to become a professional actor is equally as spontaneous. However, making a plan probably never entered your mind when you made your decision. This is why we're presenting the twelve step plan to help guide you toward your career.

Each month we will lay out new tasks for you to accomplish. You will carry the lessons learned from the previous month and use them to complete the exercises for the current month. Completing the monthly exercises in this book enables you to see how every step connects. What you accomplish the month or week before affects where and what you are doing now.

Organizing your thoughts and defining a plan doesn't mean you are conforming or limiting your choices. It simply gives you a familiar path to take—a road to follow. But *you* orchestrate the trip. Where you want to go and how you want to get there is *your* creation, just like acting.

Knowledge is power and how you use these steps will help you determine your success. If you were taking a vacation to Hawaii, you would first find out if you were traveling during the rainy season. If so, you'd pack accordingly. The same is true for acting. A *Twelve Step Plan To Becoming An Actor In LA* will help you gauge what you need to take with you and what to expect when you arrive.

As a newcomer, you will encounter obstacles and disappointments. You need to know that hundreds of thousands of people come to Los Angeles each year to pursue the same dream. Some return home, some will find a different career, but the survivors will constantly find new ways to succeed as actors. We cannot keep you from making choices that are perhaps not the most advantageous, but we can minimize the pitfalls by giving you the tools to keep your career moving forward.

Never be discouraged to the point where you give up or think you are a failure. This is an easy trap to fall into. You see money and success and people around you who appear to be "making it." You wonder if it's ever going to happen for you. The truth may be it's not your time yet. Know that your time may come tomorrow—not out of luck or chance—but out of preparation and working the steps we are providing for you.

Our belief is that anyone can create and maintain an acting career. Know who you are and where you fit in. One of the most important areas this book will help you in is Casting.

How does a casting director, producer or director see you? Start asking yourself, "What actors do I relate to?" When you see a movie, what characters are you drawn to where you say, "I can play that role now, not in twenty years, but today." If you look and behave more like Drew Carey than Tom Cruise, you won't be considered for the romantic lead—even though you may be quite romantic. Your romance is a quality that can be put into your characters. It is something special to you. But how you appear and behave does not fit that particular role. Like pieces in a puzzle, you need to know what role(s) fit. This may sound simple, but when this connection is made, careers have been launched.

There is the art of acting and then there is the art of becoming an actor—know both well. Learn as Stanislavsky said, "…to love the art in yourself not yourself in the art…" Keep the spark that motivates you alive each and every step of the way and believe in your ability to make this dream a reality.

Below are the twenty questions you need to ask yourself before you embark on becoming a professional actor in LA.

❏ Why do I want to be an actor?

❏ Why do I think acting is the career for me?

❏ What do I get from being an actor?

❏ Does rejection fuel my fire?

❏ What genres do I like and why?

❏ What is my type? Am I willing to keep reinventing myself?

❏ How accessible are my emotions to me? To others?

❏ Do I feel acting will heal me? How?

❏ How can I use fear to motivate me in a constructive way?

❏ How do I know I have the focus and obsession to succeed?

❏ What aspect of myself do I feel best expresses me?

❏ What does success mean to me?

❏ What career would I choose other than acting?

❏ How is my voice unique?

❏ Am I able to detach from my roles? How?

❏ Am I using acting as a platform to display my own emotional difficulty? How?

❏ Am I willing to completely expose myself?

❏ What do I think it means to be an actor?

❏ Do I often feel I could perform roles better than the actors I see?

❏ At this point in my life, do I feel I need to do this?

If you had no trouble answering at least 16 out of the 20 questions, you are ready to take the next step to pursuing a professional career as an actor.

CHAPTER 1

Step One, Month One

Preparing Your Journey

> "A journey of a thousand miles begins with just one step."
> —Anonymous

DORI KELLER

I had what I thought was a vision, a germ of an idea where everything would fall into place. I had recently graduated from the acting program at the State University of New York at Purchase. Like most of my friends, I was working in a restaurant in Manhattan. The city where I grew up felt too imposing, almost impenetrable. There appeared to be an invisible wall surrounding the acting/theater community. It was a castle, which for me, as a young adult, felt daunting. I didn't know how to cross the moat and into the "kingdom." I believed that if I stayed in New York, the excitement and drive to become an actor would die. I was faced with a dilemma, a decision, a career choice. Acting was my chosen career, and I was willing to do whatever I had to bring this dream to fruition.

After a month of planning, I left New York on January 7th, 1981. I took the next Tower Air Flight out and landed in LA. I stayed with my brother and sister-in-law in a determined quest to pursue acting.

The concept of being able to move to a new city and work as an actor originated while I was studying acting at Purchase. While learning what seemed more like "academic acting," I was fortunate to have started working professionally at the Williamstown Theater Festival in Massachusetts during the summer. To be honest, I went to Williamstown for two reasons. The first reason was that Williamstown was the country's most renowned regional summer theater. The second reason was I heard an actress, whom I admired, regularly performed there. At the age of 18, I had an unbelievable crush on Blythe Danner—a wonderful actress, whom to this day, I feel is one of the preeminent performers in America. So it was the reputation of the theater and the lure of meeting a woman I not only admired as an artist, but was also secretly in love with that started me on my path to being a professional actor.

The expectations and hopes I had for that summer came to fruition. I met Blythe and found her as wonderful and sincere in person as she was on stage and film. I also worked with and developed relationships with other actors, writers, and directors; some of who now live and work in Los Angeles. People who have remained in my life and to this day I consider good friends.

It was this experience, which led me to LA the summer before my graduation. It was an experiment. I would learn the lay of the land, see what was what, and discover if I could fit into a world that was completely different from the one where I grew up.

It was never a thought-out plan. It never evolved to the point where I said this is what I am doing and this is how I am going to do it. I operated from instinct. I traveled around town, saw areas I did and did not want to live in, and explored potential job possibilities both in and out of acting. I also joined an acting class to study my craft as well as meeting actor friends who could teach me about the business on the West Coast.

During the previous two years at Williamstown, I was fortunate to have become friends with Bruce Paltrow whom I later learned, was the creator and producer of *The White Shadow* and *St. Elsewhere*. Bruce was extremely generous with me with regard to his time and knowledge. And for a period of my life, I considered him my mentor.

He invited me to the studio and gave me free reign to observe the filming of his shows. Those three months were invaluable. I spent most of my time on the lot, watching, learning, and when I was ready, lucked in and received a small part in *The White Shadow*, which allowed me to become a member of the Screen Actors Guild.

I knew the opportunity and the relationship I had developed was special, something that did not come around every day. Bruce was the first person in the business to give me a shot. He introduced me to the business of television and how series were developed, filmed, and produced. For all the lessons I learned, I will always be grateful.

Several people gave me the names of teachers and acting studios to visit. The most important suggestion came from Blythe who recommended Milton Katselas. He had directed her on Broadway in the play *Butterflies Are Free*. Moreover, she said he was a director and teacher of the first order. I set up an appointment and interviewed for his class. By the end of the meeting, I knew I would return to LA and study with a man named Katselas. It turns out that Blythe's suggestion led me to one of the most influential relationships in my development as an artist and human being.

I had a mission, to become a professional actor. This need drove every choice I made, including the books I read, the movies I saw, and the plays in New York where I would wait backstage to meet the actors and talk with them about their performance.

My plan included immersing myself into everything related to acting. This meant learning more about myself and the world around me through art, history, philosophy, and political science. It meant reading the newspaper, watching the news and reading magazines—all with the goal to expand and understand more about life and art.

Actors can be very self-centered; but the artist must be interested in the world and people around him, not just his own reflections. He has to be open to the experience and knowledge of writers, painters, poets, the man behind the bar, even the women sitting next to them on the bus or subway. This may seem more intellectual than actively creating and doing a plan. However, your plan must be based not only on you as an actor but also on you as a human being.

Who you are and what you are about is what is going to make you interesting to people. Directors, agents, and managers want to see more than the actor when you audition. They want to know if there is a person behind the reading. People are interesting; actors can be boring.

While reading this and the succeeding chapters, use the work pages provided to begin compiling a list of relationships and potential contacts. Keep a log of everyone you have met, their name, number, a brief description of who they are and, if need be, what they look like. You'll be surprised how often you'll see a name in your book and forget where you met them or what you talked about. Little hints of where you were, whom you were with, or what even they were wearing will bring everything back and can be used for later conversations.

This list will also come in handy when you meet someone that also knows them—and you will. This may seem like a very large city and an overpopulated industry, but the truth is quite the opposite. The longer you are here, the more you see how small the entertainment community really is. Think of it as a large high school where word travels fast and where everyone knows everyone else's business. You will be surprised when someone you've just met tells you that they've heard your name mentioned around town.

It is true there are "six degrees of separation" between people and events. However, it's all a part of your plan to expand your relationships and expand your knowledge and understanding of the business and art.

DAWN LERMAN

I had no plan. No idea why I wanted to be an actress. I just knew that I felt deeply and was highly sensitive and emotional. I misinterpreted my pain as talent. I wanted to run from where I came and run to the dream of fame, acceptance, and unconditional love. I had no place to live, no transportation, no driver's license, only the number of a guy whom I met at a party who had promised me the world.

To my credit, I had studied in New York under the direction of Jack Waltzer, whom I was referred to by Arthur Miller. I had the incredible opportunity to audition for Mr. Miller when he was casting the Broadway production of *Death of a Salesman* with Dustin Hoffman. This was my first audition and after several bad line readings, Mr. Miller said that I was just about the worst actress he'd ever seen. However, he did say that I had that "special look" in my eyes, a quality similar to the first time he met Marilyn. So, while I couldn't act, I had the pain of a legend. This fueled my excitement and my inherent naiveté. I just knew I was going to be discovered.

However, what I lacked in my impulsive trip to LA was knowledge, a plan, and a sense of who I was as an actress, as well as responsibility and defined long and short-term goals. In addition to these things, I also lacked the tangible things like transportation, an apartment, friends, and any family blessings. I didn't take myself or my acting seriously. But to have a career as an actor, you must take it seriously and have a plan, a step-by-step building plan—a plan not that different from those of my friends who took conventional entry-level jobs after college. They didn't take these jobs because they were exciting; they took them because they were part of a building block plan for ascending the corporate ladder. They were starting at A in order to get to Z. They were working hard and paying their dues in order to learn their business. Acting is also a business, but I chose it as a rebellion and an escape. Therefore, I could have no long-term success as an actress. I wanted to go directly to Z without ever touching A. However, like building a house, you must lay down a foundation before you can build the top floor. So, while my luck was good, my foundation was a little shaky.

My first break was renting a guesthouse from Melissa Gilbert. Her mother, Barbara Gilbert, lived in the main house and was an influential Hollywood agent. She adopted me as one of her own. She was amazing. A couple of weeks after I moved in, Barbara got me in the door of every major casting call in town. I was given a shot a number of times and made an impression. I was called back and met the producers on some big projects. People thought I had a quality. I also lacked a quality—confidence. I constantly apologized for who I was or for even being in the room.

While the feedback I received on my acting was good, the underlying message that always came across was the same. Namely, that I didn't believe in my work and myself. I looked to agents, casting directors, and producers to validate me. But that's not their job; their job is to hire you because you are the best person for the role. They need to count on you to deliver a vision. The very reasons I wanted to become an actress are the very reasons that stifled my career. Believe in yourself first before you ask someone else to believe in you.

As you've read, Dori's and my experiences of moving to LA were quite different. But what we share is a full-circle understanding of what it takes to establish and maintain a career as a professional in LA. Below are the essential steps for month one.

Essentials For Month One

1. Before going any further, take time to answer or reassess the questions you answered in the introduction. Don't go any further until you're sure this is the career you want. If you're waffling, wait. Take more classes, talk to someone who knows the industry, and talk to someone you trust—a teacher, a counselor, a family member, a friend. For those of you who believe now is the time, begin taking the steps.

2. If you can, plan a trip with a friend before the actual move. It will make the city more familiar and the relocation easier.

3. Write down your goals for the month.

4. Write down the people you know (friends of friends) who live in LA.

5. Make calls ahead of time. Let people know you're coming and what your goals are when you arrive. Create a mission statement that clearly defines what you want to accomplish during the visit.

6. Tour the city. This means taking out a map, a *Thomas Guide,* which you can purchase at any bookstore. Block off areas on the map that are within your price range and that are conveniently located. The best way to find an apartment is to walk through neighborhoods where you want to live. There are usually signs outside. If you have the means for a cell phone and a car, then you could even drive through various neighborhoods calling the signs as you see them. A standard lease is six to twelve months. There is a free telephone service that provides information on rentals all over the LA area: dial your LA area code + 789-RENT.

7. Obtain transportation. If possible when you arrive, rent a car. LA is not a walking city. You'll only need those Reeboks for the gym, which you'll need a car to get to. Taxis are expensive and most public transportation is slow. However, there is now a Metro Line, which goes from downtown to North Hollywood with stops at Wilshire, Vermont, Hollywood & Vine, Hollywood & Highland and Universal City. If you can't rent a car, then work out ahead of time how you can get access to a car.

8. Make appointments ahead of time to interview with acting teachers and schools. If you don't have immediate access to a list, you can refer to Chapter 4. These are our picks of the best schools and teachers. Talk to your contacts and get their recommendations as well. Finding a teacher is very personal. See if your college or university has an alumni organization

located in LA. They can make your transition much easier, especially if they are a strong organization.

9. Pursue any job leads that might come up in conversation. It also doesn't hurt to ask friends and relatives if they know someone who might help you.

10. Set up auditions with theater companies in town. This is a good way of getting involved quickly and developing new relationships. Refer to Chapter 11 for the application and interviewing process. Each company will have their own requirements for interviews.

11. For those of you who have graduated from conservatories where you auditioned for agents, managers, and casting directors, try to arrange appointments with their LA affiliates. Not all agencies work out of both coasts, but most have sister agencies in LA. This is also true of Chicago and Miami, which are constantly attracting new talent and business.

12. Check out where the best places are for your hobbies. It is very important to have as balanced a life as possible. Remember, you want to be more than just an actor.

13. Surf the internet for the best airfares. Don't forget hotwire.com, travelocity.com, and priceline.com. There are always great deals. You can also call **Cheap Tickets** 1-800-377-1000 or **Cheap Seats** 1-800-451-7200 for the cheapest fares. Travel Associates can get you a ticket on American with only a three day advance. 5550 Wilshire Blvd. (323) 933-7388

14. Before you arrive, check the weather. Sounds stupid, but it can surprise you.

15. When you arrive, buy a copy of the *Hollywood Reporter* and *Daily Variety*. These are industry trade papers geared toward the business of show business. The industry has its own language, and this is a good way to get familiar with how people write and speak about the industry.

16. At the end of the week, pick up a copy of *Back Stage West*. It comes out weekly and has casting notices for film, TV, and stage. Go to the nearest Starbuck's or Coffee Bean and enjoy a frappacino—it's the "in" drink. You'll be surprised how many actors you'll meet. This is a good place to shmooze and get leads on jobs, housing, and what's generally happening in town (i.e. bars, music, clubs, etc.).

17. If you are looking for a car, furniture, or virtually anything used, pick up a copy of *The Recycler*, or head to…Beverly Hills for garage sales and thrift stores. Also The National Council For Jewish Women 323-651-2930 has the best thrift stores throughout the city. N.C.J.W. also has a free counseling talk line for women (Women Helping Women) 323-655-3807. Desperate men can also call. In addition they have two fabulous flea markets each year. Don't miss the **Melrose Trading Post**, a fabulous flee market, for the hip and groovy crowd. Meets every Sunday in the parking lot at Fairfax High School

located on Melrose and Fairfax.

18. Visit the main office of the *Screen Actors Guild* and look at their main board. Not only does it list casting, but also lists available apartments and apartments swaps. Do the same at *Actors' Equity* and *American Federation of TV and Radio Artists*. You don't need to be a member to check out the boards.

19. Start looking for a job immediately. The money you brought out will go quicker than you think. If your family can help out while you're getting settled, great, have this discussion beforehand.

20. Get a list of temp agencies if you are skilled at office and reception work. The hours are flexible and the pay is based on your skills. If you want to learn how studios operate, you can try to get temporary work at one of the studios. This is a good way to get on the lot and have lunch at the commissary. You never know who you'll meet. The first six months are about setting up a life, a routine, and further developing your craft. You want to learn the business. Other recommended jobs are: assistant to producers, directors, managers, talent agents, and casting directors. Through osmosis, you'll learn about the business from a different vantage points.

You are now on your way. You are beginning to formulate your plan. The following pages will help you further assess reassess, and define your goals.

Goal Worksheet

- *What were your goals for the month?*

- *What have you accomplished in the last 30 days?*

- *What have you not accomplished and reasons why not?*

- *What are your goals for the next 30 days?*

- *When you get frustrated, what helps to relax you?*

- *Do you have a friend or partner on this journey?*

List twenty adjectives that best describe how you feel about your progress this month:

1-	*11-*
2-	*12-*
3-	*13-*
4-	*14-*
5-	*15-*
6-	*16-*
7-	*17-*
8-	*18-*
9-	*19-*
10-	*20-*

Negative thoughts you need to let go of:

Things that you are grateful for that happened this month:

Budget Worksheet

Essentials to budget and save for prior to moving and living in LA

❑ *Transportation to LA*

❑ *Transportation in LA (car, rental, gas, insurance, registration)*

❑ *Rent (to be safe, have enough for first, last, a security deposit, and a two months rent).*

❑ *Utilities (phone, water and power, etc.).*

❑ *Necessary expenses (answering service, beeper, cell phone (optional), trade subscriptions, books, etc.)*

❑ *Resume and headshots (even if you have them already, you'll probably want to get them redone).*

❑ *Classes and workshops*

❑ *Food and entertainment*

❑ *Health insurance (available through SAG—if you are a member and meet the earning quota.)*

❑ *Emergency funds (for the inevitable but unseen)*

❑ *Clothing*

❑ *Furniture (you can find furnished apartments, but you may want to get your own stuff—it's cheaper especially if you go to flea markets, tag sales, The Salvation Army and garage sales. There are no shortages of tag sales in LA)*

❑ *Once again, this depends on your style and, how much preparation you have done before you come to LA, and where you're going to live.*

Contact Worksheet

NAME	COMPANY	TITLE	PHONE	ADDRESS

Packing Worksheet

KEY THINGS TO BRING:

- ❑ *Driver's license*

- ❑ *Passport*

- ❑ *Headshots and resumes*

- ❑ *Contact numbers*

- ❑ *Variety of winter and summer clothing (Really, it can get cold in LA, especially in the mountains)*

- ❑ *Shoes*

- ❑ *Books, Journals*

- ❑ *Familiar keepsakes from home*

- ❑ *Sleeping bag*

- ❑ *Toiletries*

- ❑ *Makeup*

- ❑ *Money*

- ❑ *Credit Cards*

- ❑ *Social Security Card*

- ❑ *Health Insurance Card*

Emotional Worksheet

"What do I need to bring in my emotional suitcase?"
Everyone's journey is different as well as everyone's individual needs.

Write 20-50 adjectives or qualities you will need to become successful on your move to LA.

Example: For my journey, I need strength, confidence and support from my family.

- _____
- _____
- _____
- _____
- _____
- _____
- _____
- _____
- _____
- _____
- _____
- _____
- _____
- _____
- _____
- _____
- _____
- _____
- _____
- _____
- _____
- _____

CHAPTER 2

Month Two: Step Two

Learning Los Angeles and Setting Up Your New Life

> "All journeys have secret destinations of which the traveler is unaware"
> —Martin Buber

DAWN

"Oh my God! Where am I? How did I get here? Did I really make the right choice? And why does everyone look so perfect?"

More than a few of these questions echoed in my mind, as a twenty-two year old hopeful, looking to stake my claim as an actress in Hollywood.

The first discovery I made during this period of adjustment was that I was not blond, tall or tan. I am not telling you I never looked at myself in the mirror or when I did saw someone other then myself standing in front of me. I knew I was a small, Jewish girl from New York who, until now, always fit in with her surroundings.

I also knew Los Angeles as the land of hope and plenty. However, I never expected to see so many people fighting to appear more perfect than the next. Everyone seemed to be a variation of a single theme. All the people looked and dressed as if they walked out of an ad for either GQ or Victoria's Secret. I felt as if I walked out of the film *Honey, I Shrunk The Kids*—and I was the kid.

To help revive my dwindling spirits, I withdrew twenty dollars from my fanny pack. I had $280.00 left to my name, but I needed to splurge my wealth on discovering the sights and adventures of LA.

I quickly learned that Los Angeles is not a walking town. Without a car, a person can only travel so far. You will learn, sooner or later, exactly how vast LA is and how much of this sprawling metropolis is not walker friendly.

On this particular day in Hollywood, I quickly became parched from the intense sunlight and heat. It was still only 11 o'clock in the morning. I stopped at the first familiar landmark I could find—the local McDonald's. The Golden

Arches quickly soothed my frayed nerves. From that moment on, the house that Ronald built became a psychological oasis wherein I could re-evaluate my next step.

A few hours later, it was time to caffeine my body with a tall iced coffee. However, I was horrified to learn that no one knew the whereabouts of a coffee shop. New Yorkers learn at an early age that coffee shops, (this was before Starbucks or the Coffee Bean) are cloned every 30 seconds and nest every half a block.

I did not look as if I were from a different world although I felt like I came from Mars. It seemed as if people spoke a different language. I was a pioneer, an East Coast adventurer willing to brave a sunny, multi-ethnic, highway infested, strip mall, megalopolis. Where was the glamorous Hollywood I saw on Entertainment Tonight? Where could a girl like me get discovered drinking a tall iced coffee?

Rather my first discovery was that I needed a car, some driving lessons (some say I still do), and a map to get me around town.

The first leg of my quest led me to an outdoor newsstand near the Las Palmas Theater in the heart of Hollywood. This I related to; they had the *New York Post*, a hometown newspaper. It was not the *New York Times*, but at least I knew what they were talking about. Here was a paper filled with something other than stories about 'road rage,' 'SIG alerts,' and 'car jacking.'

It was among the familiar magazines that I discovered a local paper called the *Recycler*, a weekly-classified paper. I flipped to the used car section and found (pinch me I'm dreaming) a $200.00 used 1976 Toyota Celica.

Had my luck changed? Were the universal powers now shining their divine light on me? To reach the state of bliss I now longed for, I knew I needed to travel; but how long would it take me to reach my Celica. I learned my chariot to Nirvana was in the **Valley**. The owner told me it was only a few minutes from Hollywood—by car—but he did not tell me how long by bus. "No rest for the weary," I said as I started on my journey.

The City of Los Angeles provided public transportation that seemed not only reliable but also a good way to meet real Angelenos. But I learned that taking the bus was tantamount to having my passport stamped for passage into some Third World purgatory nation where no one spoke the same language. There was Chinese, Japanese, Korean, German, Philippine, Thai, and Spanish—not high school Spanish mind you—which would have made my life a little easier. No. This was street Spanish, a new language filled with slang and mutations of words and phrases I never heard. Gone was the security I felt only moments before where people could actually say "coffee shop, huh?" To my current Hell of "Donde esta bla bla bla…?" Why didn't I pay closer attention in school? Where was my English-Spanish, Spanish-English dictionary I erroneously mocked in high school?

As the bus labored up **Highland Ave**—aptly named for its spectacular view of the Holiday Inn, the Ripley's Believe It or Not Museum, and assorted other Hollywood attractions—I was experiencing Los Angeles first hand and was setting up my life as a successful actress in LA. Over the loud speaker, I suddenly heard, "…**Hollywood Bowl** next stop…" Now we are getting some place. I can learn the lay of the land and see the sights without having to become one of the sights. This was fantastic and also much cheaper. I sat and waited for the sounds of his mellifluous voice to continue—nothing. I desperately yearned for the driver to give me a guided voice—over tour of the area, to tell me stories of the great musicians who played just up the road, around that bend and beyond those trees; but the closest I got was the electric sign thanking the public for another successful summer.

I was on my own and took to watching the street signs to find where I was going. The different voices and languages flew around the confines of the bus as it chugged up the hill and across the **Cahuenga** (pronounced ka-wang-a) pass into what is termed the "**Valley**."

When we reached the crest of the mountain and began our descent, I finally saw it—the Valley!! I was transfixed. Then mysteriously, I found myself being transported into some Bob Hope, Bing Crosby road movie where "Thank You For The Memories" played softly over my view of what is fondly referred to as "the other city".

I knew that just around that bend, over that hill and past those trees, Steven Spielberg was working. It's where I also heard that some of the great movies of our time were created; i.e., *Psycho, Jaws, Lethal Weapon, Batman,* etc. Beyond the bluff and traffic to my right, acting thrived and art was created. I made a mental note to myself, "Remember how to get here for auditions." Finally, a sign said, "**Welcome To Universal City**."

I was feeling safe and knew I was now on my way. That was until a voice stated flatly, "Last stop, transfer to the 10." Terror struck, I was like a rabbit trapped in the headlights of an on coming car. Transfer? Where? How? What am I going to do? I tried to relax and referred to a book I bought at **LAX**—*LA and Zen and $10 a Day*. It cryptically said that the answers to those questions, even those that hadn't been asked, would be revealed to me at the appropriate time. I exited the bus, walked strong of foot, full of determination, transfer in hand to the next stop, and waited. New Yorkers have a manic sense of time. If you don't hear or see something coming down the tracks or street in five minutes or less, then you're doomed.

I took advantage of my new found survival skills and read another street sign— Vineland…I dropped my gaze and right below, a sign read Studio Coffee Shop. Here I could finally get my tall iced coffee and maybe get discovered.

By this time the line for the bus, which I was still expecting to arrive at any moment, got longer and longer until it wrapped around itself like a snake. The time, however, was well spent. I was processing information left and right about the Valley. I even learned a great deal about driving by watching the traffic back up to what amounted to a slow crawl. What was the problem? Had there been an accident or, possibly a concert at the Universal Amphitheater? Neither, people were trying to enter and exit the Freeway, but why so many cars all of a sudden? The woman next to me belligerently said it was the start of rush hour traffic and that now we were really screwed. It couldn't be rush hour I proudly announced; it was only 3:30 in the afternoon. A look of pity crawled, like the traffic, across the woman's face and she went back to fanning herself.

The next leg of my trip took me through other parts of the Valley like Studio City. I remember hearing one of my New York friends say there was another film and television studio somewhere around here. The bus stopped at the Corner of Ventura and Radford. To my left was another McDonald's in a large shopping center and to my right I noticed the **Samuel French Theater Bookstore**. Another place I need to remember. I looked back as the bus pulled away from the curb and saw that just down Radford past the trees and over a large brick wall was a studio, the **CBS Radford Studio** to be exact.

I was a little confused because I was not completely sure where I was headed, and I knew I needed to go west. At least that's what the Celica man told me. The person sitting across the aisle reassured me we were in fact going west, west on **Ventura Blvd.** through Studio City and into **Sherman Oaks**. I told him I was new to the city and was on my way to buy my first car. He gave me a good piece of advice about driving through the city. "You know you're going north when the mountains are in front of you. You know you are going west when they are to the right and you know you are going south when you go over the hill to what we refer to as the basin and the hill is behind you."

The bus ambled along **Ventura Blvd.** through **Sherman Oaks**, which seemed like a very nice community to live. It was packed with restaurants, clothing stores, music and video stores, even small shops that reminded me of those little out of the way places in New York. As the sun was going down, the traffic eased a bit but never really cleared. I eventually made it to **Van Nuys** and **Ventura Blvd.** From here I would walk to find my Celica man. The Celica man told me his house was only a few minutes north of the bus stop.

I picked up the pace; the anticipation of seeing the car was killing me. One block, two blocks, suddenly it was turning into seven and eight blocks and these were not New York blocks. These were real suburban blocks that could stretch at least a quarter of a mile at a time. The temperature on a bank clock said it was 92° degrees. The exact time was lost when I finally found my Celica street, and at last I reached the house—a simple ranch style, one story home, pleasant, well kept. The aura, like it said in the Zen book felt right, but where was the car, where was the car? I rang the doorbell and after some time, a man stuck his head out.

I was escorted to the back, past a couple of pit bulls chained to a tree. They seemed to be at a safe distance, but I noticed the animals had chewed through a nice portion at the base and had made good progress on another side.

In spite of that, I clung to my hope, my dream, and my wish that I did not have to take the bus back to Hollywood. I could go in style by Celica. The light went on in the garage and there sat a dirty blue, two-toned vehicle with a look that told me it had been great once—an old warrior waiting for another chance to prove itself. The owner said someone was on his or her way, so if I wanted the car, I needed to pay him now. $200.00. I turned on the ignition; it started. He handed me the registration papers. I was now an official car owner. I looked at my almost depleted fanny pack and drove off. This was the beginning of my new life.

After an excruciating time of trying to find my way on to the freeway, I headed south on the 405—a.k.a. the **San Diego Freeway**, mother of all roadways in Southern California. This piece of pavement, if you take south for two hours, puts you right into San Diego—hence the name.

The traffic whizzed by faster than I ever imagined, four lanes in both directions—and every lane was the fast lane. I had no idea where I was going. I'd never driven on the freeway before and the craziness of the road made me yearn for the safety of the bus. Signs went by with names that weren't familiar—**Mulholland, Getty Circle, Sunset**—I finally took the exit that said **Beverly Hills.**I went east because the sun was now behind me and Hollywood was east, away from the beach. **Olympic Blvd.** took me through **West LA** into Beverly Hills—all very nice neighborhoods until I reached a familiar street, **Highland Avenue**. This is where I first started my journey. I drove up the street through a beautiful section of town called **Hancock Park** and into **Hollywood**. There was the McDonald's—my oasis. I drove past it towards my new home in Los Angeles.

DORI

There are easier ways to acquaint yourself with LA than the way Dawn did. Therefore, we're including a list of car rental companies and insurance agencies. Do not take risks like she did. Be a smart safe driver, buy insurance, and have a mechanic look at your car before buying it. People in LA can drive fast and sloppy, so be careful and keep your eyes on the road even though there are many distractions.

The Twenty Questions You Need to Ask Yourself to Start Your New Life in LA

❑ Do I have a place to live?

❑ Do I have transportation?

❑ If I have a car, have I registered my car, purchased insurance, and obtained a smog check?

❑ Do I have a *Thomas Guide?*

❑ Have I familiarized myself with the different areas of LA?

❑ Do I have a job?

❑ Do I have enough money saved for the next two months?

❑ Have I begun to fill my contact worksheet?

❑ Do I have any support network; i.e., friends, family, or classes?

❑ Have I begun to investigate different classes and workshops in town?

❑ Do I have an answering service, voice mail, pager or answering machine?

❑ Do I have a good headshot and resume and at least 100 copies?

❑ Have I visited Samuel French Bookstore and stocked up on plays and scene books?

❑ Am I allowing adequate time to take care of myself?

❑ Am I looking at all the acting trades weekly?

❑ Have I met anyone working in the business?

❑ Have I gone to any on-camera-auditioning workshop?

❑ Have I contacted all the people I was told by my friends and family to call when I arrive in LA?

❑ Am I beginning to establish a routine?

❑ Have I explored any of the local hot spots?

SPECIAL TIP
...DO YOU KNOW ABOUT THE UNIONS?
....A MUST IN THIS INDUSTRY!

Unions

The bulletin boards at the following unions are great sources of information. Not only do they list all casting information, but also classes, support groups, housing, and other classified types of advertising.

AEA
(Actors' Equity Association)—
Union which covers legit theater.
5757 Wilshire Blvd.
General Info: (323) 634-1750
Hotline: (323) 634-1776 (local castings)

AFTRA
(American Federation of Television and Radio Arts)—Union which covers Radio & TV
5757 Wilshire Blvd.
General Inf.: (323) 634-8100
Hotline: (323) 634-8263
Announcements for auditions and castings)
Showcase information
(323) 634-8262

SAG
(Screen Actors Guild)—Union which covers film, commercials and TV.
5757 Wilshire Blvd.
General Info. (323) 954-1600 (membership dues, contracts, residuals.)
Hotline: (323) 937-3441 (Casting/Showcase information)
Hotline: (323) 549-6657 (SAG Film Society—must be a member to order yearly ticket package for new movie screenings.

Three SAG voucher jobs entitle background actors to SAG membership.

Our Favorite Car Insurance Companies and Brokers

The Auto Club of Southern California. Must be a member of AAA. It's well worth the membership. *(323) 525-0018*

Farmers Insurance—Dennis Sokol Sherman Oaks—If you have a decent driving record, Dennis will give you one of the best rates in town! Very personalized service *(818) 990-2954*

Geico Insurance—Services all parts of the US. Offers insurance even if you have an out of state license. *(800) 453-6445*

State Farm Insurance—Good Rates for good drivers. *(323) 549-3800*

21st Century Insurance Excellent rates for good drivers—no personal agents. *(800) 211-7283*

Broker Agents

Deals with many insurance companies in case your driving record is spotty.

George Viso Insurance *Ask* for George *(323) 655-5266* *(323) 852-6971*

Unik Insurance *(818) 766-3836* *(323) 381-7671*

Glencoe Insurance Ask for Richard or Randy. (310) 836-2770

Car Rentals that are Reasonable

Although you will have to buy at some point in the land of highways and automobiles.

Alamo—Open twenty—four hours. Discount coupons from the airlines. Special weekend rates. *(800) 327-9633* *(310) 649-9633*

Basic Rent A Car *(310) 446-9964-West LA*

(323) 463-9999-Hollywood Reasonable rates

Enterprise—Good weekend specials as well as monthly rates *(323) 938-4646* *(800) 325-8007*

The City at Large

LA is a huge multi-ethnic city with hundreds, maybe thousands, of great restaurants, bars, hotels, movie theaters, playhouses, and gyms. There are even many more horrible dives and rip-offs. Since there are so many places, there's no way that we could even list them all. However, we've put together our own actor's favorite places and a few places we like to go.

Bars and Restaurants

These places not only have good food and drinks, but they also have an atmosphere that brings together the acting and film crowd. Places come and go, so call ahead or check out the *L.A. Weekly* for the latest hot spots.

> *Warning: LA happens to be a very seductive city. Just because you adventure out every night and meet all kinds of actors, maybe a celebrity doesn't mean you will get a job. It's always important to have balance in your life. Don't spend all of your time going out. Otherwise, you will never pass Step 2. You can't rendezvous on the town without bumping into someone who claims to be an actor and has never performed on stage or screen. Set yourself apart from all the other starting actors. One day, one month at a time, work the steps, and if you find out after a couple of years that you haven't passed Step 2, then you should start looking for another line of work.*

Being an actor is acting on a stage or screen, not just calling yourself an actor. Besides you don't want to spend all your money socializing. That's money that could be going towards taking classes and checking out what is going on in the theaters and films. Spend more money on marketing yourself rather than on drinks and cover charges. Play it smart—nurse one drink at that fancy club, save your money, and you won't even have to worry about the tough LA cops pulling you over for a DUI. With this in mind, you may not want to go out. But it's a great and exciting town to explore. Go out, enjoy the city; have fun, just don't over indulge. Take control of LA; don't lose yourself in the glitter of La La Land.

> *Warning #2: If you decide to go to a place that isn't on our list, make sure you look in their window for the health department's rating. An "A" is best, but a "B" isn't too bad; but anything lower than that, you better make sure you know what you are doing. LA also has many roadside eateries. They are often derided as "roach coaches"; some deserve that name, others are cleaner than your mother's kitchen.*

Akbar—A trendy hip bar, laid back and cheap.
4356 W. Sunset Blvd., Silver Lake
(323) 665-6810.

Babe & Ricky's Inn—A classic world-renowned blues club. Originally in downtown LA for 37 yrs. it recently moved to it present location. Hot, heavy blues should carry you through the night. A must go.
4339 Leimert Blvd., Leimert Park
(323) 295-9112.

Barfly—Full of midlevel Hollywood wanna-bees it's a fun show to watch. Just don't try to get reservations. Look like you're hot and you'll probably get seated.
8730 W. Sunset Blvd., West
Hollywood
(310) 360-9490.

Backstage Café—The crowd is electric and the food is tasty, but the music is intoxicating. Go after 10pm for big band music.
9433 Brigton Way, Beverly Hills
(310) 777-0252

Cinespace
Dinner and classic movies six nights a week. Special industry events.
6356 Hollywood Blvd. Hollywood
(323) 817-film

Congo Room—Terrific Salsa Bands. Join a wonderful mixed crowd on thedance floor. Dining also available.
5364 Wilshire Blvd, L.A., Hollywood
(323) 938-1696

The Derby—Swing is king! Dances, drink, learn how to swing dance.

The line is long, but the nostalgia is worth it.
4500 Los Feliz Blvd., Los Feliz
(323) 663-8979.

Dragonfly—A spacious bar with a great outdoor patio. A great place to meet the locals. The music changes daily so call ahead.
6510 Santa Monica Blvd., Hollywood
(323) 466-6111

The Dresden—Authentic 60's Hollywood. The décor hasn't changed and neither has the house band of Marty and Elaine. You can request a song and if you want or sing along. It gets crowded so come early for a table and look like money.
1760 N. Vermont, Los Feliz
(213) 665-4294.

Dublins—An Irish pub with sports playing on every one of its twenty something TVs. Beer and wings. Great rowdy fun.
8240 W. Sunset, LA
(323)-656-0100

El Cholo—A favorite for Mexican food (originally opened in 1920)
1121 S. Western Ave.
(323) 734-2773
1025 Wilshire Blvd. @ 11th St. (new)
(310) 899-1106

El Floridita—Cuban food, Cuban music! Go with a group and don't be discouraged by the fact that it is in a strip mall.
1253 N. Vine, Hollywood
(323) 871-8612.

Formosa Cafe—A great actors hang out. Attracts all walks of life. Decadent food—definitely a great meeting place.
7156 Santa Monica Blvd. LA
(323) 850-9050

Ghengis Cohen—Very trendy, Chinese food. Separate room for club acts.
740 N. Fairfax
(323) 653-0640

Goldfingers—A fun place to listen to bands. Dancing girls in bird cages. Ultra mod bar.
6423 Yucca, Hollywood
(323) 962-2913

Gotham Hall
A very happening place for Monday night football. All the waitresses look like super models.
1431 3rd Street, Santa Monica
(310) 394-8865

Ireland's 32
Great fun. Irish actor's hangout. Bands on weekends. Casual.
13721 Burbank Boulevard, Burbank
(818) 785-4031

Good Luck—A dark bar with a Chinese theme, but more importantly a good bartender, stiff drinks, and a good place to meet the opposite sex.
1514 Hillhurst, Los Feliz
(323) 666-3524

The Joint—A great space with a cover charge. The music is rock, the drinks are strong, and the crowd is always

looking to party. A great stop-off on the way to someplace else.
8771 West Pico Blvd.
(310) 275-2619

Kareoke at the Farmer's Market— Draws a cross section of tourists and residents every Saturday.
3rd St. and Fairfax Ave.,
West Hollywood, Los Angeles.
(323) 933-9211

Katana
8439 West Sunset, West Hollywood
(323) 650-8585
Trendy crowd. Sexy outdoor terrace. Wonderful people watching. Japanese theme.

Largo—Readings, music, dinner and drinks.
432 North Fairfax Ave.
West Hollywood
(323)852-1073

Lava Lounge—An excellent pick-up place. Seating is limited, so arrive with style early and try one of the exotic drinks. Bands play here occasionally, but mostly a DJ.
1533 N. La Brea, Hollywood
(323) 876-6612

Les Deux Cafe—Very trendy. Great restaurant. Great bar, good house bands, Beautiful people. Great for celebrity watching.
1638 N. Las Palmas Ave.
(323) 465-0509

Liquid Kitty—Don't bother to dress-up, casual is the way to go. Nothing fancy or pretentious, just a straight bar. Perfect for when you just want a beer with out the attitude. Live music.
11780 W. Pico Blvd., West Los Angeles
(310) 473-3707.

Lunaria—Rest. & jazz bar. Great place for single events. Great dining & jazz. Separate room for club acts.
10351 Santa Monica Blvd.
(310) 282-8870

The Mayan Night Club
Feel as if you are on a movie set. Live salsa bands. Three floors.
1038 South Hill Street
(213) 746-4674

The Mint—Great live music, strong drinks –a fun place to meet people. Cover charge for the music.
6010 Pico Blvd., Los Angeles
(323) 954-9400

Musso & Frank's—One of the vintage hangouts for writers. Good hearty food –no California cuisine. Great martinis.
You can almost hear Glen Miller playing in the background.
6667 Hollywood Blvd., Hollywood
(323) 467-7788

The Rainbow—Rock-n–Roll all night long. Classic LA club.
9015 Sunset Blvd
(310) 278-4232

Rebecca's—Trendy Mexican Café and club. Lots of beautiful people.

101 Broadway, Santa Monica
(310) 260-1100

Sky Bar—Go before Sunset; Otherwise, unless you are a celebrity or on the guest list, you will never get in. The crowd is Euro-American. The waitresses look like super models. Have a great time while you people watch on the cushions poolside overlooking the city. Owned by Randy Gerber, Cindy Crawford's husband. Located in the Hotel Modrian.
8440 West Sunset, W. Hollywood
(323) 848-6025

Spaceland—Incredible music, a great night out.
1717 Silverlake Blvd., Silver Lake
(323) 661-4380

Sugar—Very new, very trendy, attracts the most beautiful young crowd. Funky music groups.
814 Broadway, Santa Monica
(310) 899-1989

Spago
176 North Canon Drive, Beverly Hills
(310) 385-0880
Upscale celebrity hangout.

The Viper Room—Except for one dark moment where River Phoenix died, this place is a blast, very Hollywood
8852 Sunset Blvd., West Hollywood
(310) 358-1880

After you've gotten down and dirty in the big city, most everything closes at around 1:30 am or 2:00 am. That's when you go to the late night eateries. There aren't many because people in LA like to wake up early and exercise. But there are some good places for that snack or coffee.

Late Night Eateries

Canter's Deli—open 24 hours
419 North Fairfax, West Hollywood
(323) 651-2030

Jerry's Deli—open 24 hours
12655 Ventura Blvd. Studio City
8701 Bev Blvd. Open to 3 am
(310) 289-1811

Mel's Diner—open 24 hours
8585 Sunset Blvd., West Hollywood
(310) 854-7200-4245
14846 Ventura Blvd.—open to 3 am
on weekends
(818) 990-6357

Norm's Diner—open 24 hours
470 North La Cienega, West
Hollywood
(323) 655-0167

Pink's Hot Dogs (World Famous Chili Dogs—est. 1939)
711 N. Labrea, Hollywood
(323) 931-4243

"Rock n' Roll" Denny's (Best place to see Heavy Metal heads)
Sunset Blvd., Hollywood
(323) 464-7470

Ruen Pear
5257 Hollywood Boulevard, Hollywood
(323) 466-0153
Open to 3:30am on weekends. Tasty and inexpensive Thai.

Sittons
11329 Magnolia Boulevard, Noho
(818) 761-3341
Actors hangout

Swingers
8020 Beverly Blvd., LA
(323) 653-5858

Turong Restaurant (good, inexpensive Thai)
5657 Hollywood Blvd. Hollywood
(323) 464-9074

Freeways to Remember

•2 Glendale Freeway
•5 Santa Ana Freeway/Golden State Freeway
•10 Santa Monica Freeway/San Bernardino Freeway
•60 Pomona Freeway
•90 Marina Freeway
•101 Ventura Freeway/Hollywood Freeway
•105 Glenn M. Anderson Freeway
•110 Pasadena Freeway/Harbor Freeway
•118 Simi Valley-San Fernando Valley Freeway
•210 Foothill Freeway
•405 San Diego Freeway
•605 San Gabriel River Freeway
•710 Long Beach Freeway

Getting to Know LA

Landmark Restaurants, Theaters, Clubs, Playhouses, Studios, Bookstores, and more.

HOLLYWOOD

Actor's Co-op
1760 Gower Street, Hollywood
(323) 462-8460

Actor's Gang
6209 Santa Monica Blvd., Hollywood
(323) 465-0566
Tim Robbins-Artistic Director

American Film Institute (AFI)
2021 N. Western Ave. (north of Franklin Ave).
(323) 856-7600
Accepts pictures and resumes for student films.
SAG Conservatory at AFI: on camera classes for members.

Cinegrill
Offers live entertainment nightly
7000 Hollywood Blvd. (bet. N. Highland & La Brea Ave).
(323) 466-7000
(800) 950-7667 in CA.

The Complex
6476 Santa Monica Blvd., Hollywood
(323) 645-0483

Fountain Theater
5060 Fountain Avenue, West Hollywood
(323) 663-1525

The Great American Play Series
Director—Stephan Morrow
Play readings of American classics—
must audition
(323) 462-3275

Henry Fonda Theater
6126 Hollywood Blvd. (at Gower St.)
(323) 464-0808

Highland Grounds—(coffee house,
open mike and bands nightly, a fun
easy going place to showcase.
742 North Hollywood Avenue
(323) 466-1507

Hollywood Bowl
(Bring wine, cheese and listen to the
symphony as you picnic—great
place for a romantic date)
Grounds open daily until dusk from
July through September.
2301 N. Highland Ave (at Odin St.)
(323) 850-2000

Hollywood Highland
Complex of shops, housing the
Academy Awards.
6801 Hollywood Blvd.
(323)817-0220

Hollywood Toys and Costumes
(A great place to service that inner
child of yours)
6600 Hollywood Blvd.
(213) 464-4444

Hollywood Wax Museum
(See Elvis, Marilyn and Michael
Jackson in wax)
*6767 Hollywood Blvd. (near N.
Highland Ave).*
(323) 462-8860

Hudson Theater
(4 Theaters, rest., coffee bar)
6539 Santa Monica Blvd., Hollywood
(323) 856-4249

The Ivar Theater
1605 Ivar, Hollywood
(323) 461-7300

James Doolittle Theater
(See big Broadway style plays)
*1615 N Vine St. (bet. Sunset &
Hollywood Blvd.)*
(323) 462-6666

John Anson Ford Theater
2580 N. Cahuenga Blvd
(north of the Hollywood Bowl)
(323) 461-3673

Lake Hollywood
(A reservoir in the hills. Wonderful
view of the famous "Hollywood"
sign.). Drive north on N. Cahuenga
Blvd., across Franklin Ave., right on
Dix St., left on Holly Dr., sharp right
on Deep Dell Pl., & left on Weidlake
Dr.—to arrive at the lake entrance

Larry Edmund's Bookstore
(A place to get your scene books and
stickers of agents—similar to
Samuel French)
*6644 Hollywood Blvd. (bet. Cherokee
& Whitley Ave)*
(323) 463-3273

**Los Angeles Contemporary
Exhibitions (LACE)**
(See some art and experimental performances by LA artists)
*6522 Hollywood Blvd. (bet. Wilcox St.
& Hudson Ave)*
(323) 957-1777

Los Angeles Film School
6363 West Sunset Blvd.
(323) 860-0789

Los Angeles Jewish Theater
1528 Gordon Street, Hollywood
(323) 466-0179

Magic Castle
(The mecca for all magicians, the
equivalent of the Friar's Club for
magicians)
*1999 N Sycamore Ave.(at Franklin
Ave)*
(323) 851-3313

Mann's Chinese Theater
Old theater where hand and foot-
prints of the stars—past and present
*6925 Hollywood Blvd. (bet N
Highland & N La Brea Ave).*
(323) 464-8111

Musso and Frank Grill
Oldest restaurant in Hollywood. Get
the Orson Wells booth and have a
gin and tonic or try the waffles for
breakfast.
*6667 Hollywood Blvd.(at Cherokee
Ave)*
(323) 467-7788

Pacific El Capitan Theater
(A beautiful classy, legendary
Disney-run theater. Best place to see
a Disney animated movie in LA)
*6838 Hollywood Blvd. (At N
Highland Ave).*
(323) 467-7674

Pantages Theater
*6233 Hollywood Blvd. (bet. Argyle
Ave. & Vine St.).*
(323) 468-1770

Paramount Pictures
*5555 Melrose Ave (bet. Van Ness Ave
and Gower St.)*
(323) 956-5000

Samuel French Theater Bookstore
7623 West Sunset Blvd—Hollywood
(323) 876-0570

Stages Trilingual Theater
*1540 N McCadden Pl. (off Sunset
Blvd.)*
(323) 463-5356 General information
(323) 465-1010 Box office

**August Strinberg Society of Los
Angeles**
David Patch Artistic Director
(323) 463-7525
Brunch served at play readings

Theater of Note
Membership company. Original and
innovative works.
1517 Cahuenga Blvd., Hollywood
(323) 856-8611

Theatre West
3333 Cahuenga Blvd. West
(323) 851-4839

Yamashiro Restaurant
(Sushi and other Japanese food high
up in the hills—$$$$)
*1999 N Sycamore Ave (at Franklin
Ave)*
(323) 466-5125

DOWNTOWN

Ahmanson Theater
135 North Grand Ave.
(213) 628-2772

Central Library (free cultural programs)
630 West Fifth—LA
(213) 228-7000
(213) 228-7025

Convention Center
12015 Figueroa—LA
(213) 741-1151

Dorothy Chandler Pavilion
135 North Grand Ave
(213) 972-7211

LA Philharmonic Associates
Walt Disney Concert Hall
151 South Grand
(323) 850-2000
(213) 972-7300 (Administrative Offices)

Mark Taper Theater
Auditions held monthly.
125 North Grand Ave.
(213) 628-2772
(213) 972-7374 (casting office)
(213) 972-7235 (casting hotline)

Staples Center
Where the Lakers play
1111 South Figueroa
(213) 742-7300

University of Southern Cal (USC)
Noted for its Film & TV Dept.
University Park campus—South of downtown
(213) 740-8358 (Film Department)
(213) 740-2895 (Student Production Office. Accepts pictures and resumes).
(213) 821-2744 (Theater Department)

WEST HOLLYWOOD AND ADJACENT AREAS

CBS Television City
7800 Beverly Blvd.
(323) 575-2458
Ticket information for seats for live tapings.

Château Marmont Hotel
(Belushi died here and celebs party here)
8221 Sunset Blvd.
(off Crescent Heights Blvd).
(323) 656-1010
(800) 242-8328

Coast Playhouse
8325 Santa Monica Blvd.
(323) 650-8507

Comedy Store
8433 Sunset Blvd. (off N. La Cienega Blvd)
(323) 656-6225

Coronet Theater
366 North La Cienega Blvd., West Hollywood
(310) 657-7377

Court Theatre
722 North La Cienega Blvd. West Hollywood
(310) 652-4035

Directors Guild of America
7920 Sunset Blvd. (off N Fairfax Ave)
(310) 289-2000

Doug Weston's Troubador
9081 Santa Monica Blvd. (at Doheny Drive).
(310) 276-6168

Fred Segal
8100 Melrose Ave (at Crescent Heights Blvd.).
(323) 651-4129
(Lunch, shopping and Celebs—a must)

Groundlings Theater
7307 Melrose Ave (at Poinsettia Pl).
(323) 934-9700

Greenway Court Theater
544 North Fairfax
(323) 655-7679
Free staged readings of new plays.
Open mike for original poetry
Tuesday nights.

The Grove
3rd and Fairfax (near Farmer's Market)
(323) 900-8080
Upscale complex of store, restaurants and movie theaters. Free outdoor musical events on weekends.

House of Blues
8430 Sunset Blvd. (off Olive Dr)
(323) 848-5100

Improv
8162 Melrose Ave.
(323) 651-2583

Los Angeles County Museum of Art (LACMA)
Film Dept.
5905 Willshire Blvd.
(323) 857-6000
Friday Nite Outdoor Jazz Concerts
Friday Nite Film Series

Masquers Café
8334 W. 3rd Street
(323)653-4848
(theater—casual dining)

Matrix Theater Company
7657 Merlrose Ave (bet. Stanley & Spaulding Ave)
(323) 852-1445

Pink's Famous Chili Dogs
711 N La Brea Ave (at Melrose Ave).
(323) 931-4223
Open 7:00 am-3:00 am on weekends

Roxy
9009 West Sunset Blvd.
(310) 276-2222
Famous rock bands

Sunset Plaza
8589-8720 Sunset Blvd. (between N La Cienega & N San Vincente Blvd.).
(310) 652-7137

Virgin Records Mega store, Buzz
Coffee, Wolfgang Puck Café,
Crunch Gym, and movie theaters
8000 Sunset Blvd.
*Between Laurel Ave.and Crescent
Heights Blvd.*

Writers Guild of America
7000 W. 3rd St.
(323) 951-4000

Whiskey
*1200 N. Alta Loma Rd, West
Hollywood*
(310) 657-1333

Zephyr Theatre
7458 Melrose Ave.
(323) 852-9111
(323) 852-1445

BEVERLY HILLS—CENTURY CITY—WESTWOOD

The Academy Of Motion Picture
Arts and Sciences
8949 Wilshire Blvd., Beverly Hills
(310) 247-3600

The Beverly Hills Playhouse
254 S. Robertson
(310) 855-1556

Canon Theater
205 North Canon Drive
(310) 859-2830

Freud Theater
(affiliated w/U.C.L.A. School of
Theatre, Film and Television—
located on the U.C.L.A.
Campus–Westwood
(310) 825-5761

The Geffen Playhouse
Affiliated with U.C.L.A.
10886 Le Conte—Westwood
(310) 208-5454

The Getty Museum
1200 Getty Center Drive
(310) 440-7330

The James Bridges Theater
NE Corner of UCLA
Campus–Westwood
Sunset & Hilgard
(310) 206-8013 (Archives)
(310) 206-FILM

Museum of Tolerance
9786 West Pico
(310) 553-8403

Rodeo Collection
421 N. Rodeo Drive, Beverly Hills
(310) 273-2105

The Shubert Theater
2020 Ave. of the Stars, Century City
(800) 233-3123

Writers Guild Theatre—Special
screenings for actors and directors
135 Doheny, Beverly Hills
(310) 248-2341

VENICE, SANTA MONICA AND CULVER CITY

Chaya Brasserie
8741 Alden drive
LA CA
(310) 859-8833

Culver Sony Studios
9336 Washington Blvd.
(310) 244-4000

Figtree
Venice (corner of Paloma)
(310) 392-4937
Great organic food on the boardwalk

Hals Restaurant
1349 Abbot Kinney Blvd., Venice
(310) 396-3105

Hama Restaurant
(Incredible sushi where I had my
first date with my husband to be)
Winward Circle, Venice
(310) 396-8783

L.A. Theater Works Box Office
681 Venice Blvd.—Venice
(310) 827-0809
Prod. Help at Skirball Cultural Center
2701 North Sepulveda, Brentwood
(310) 440-4500

Main Street
South of Santa Monica, once called
Ocean Park, now a trendy area for
several blocks.

Montana Ave
There are a lot of good artsy shops
on this avenue

The Novel Cafe
212 Pier Ave., Santa Monica
(310) 396-8566

Odyssey Theater
2055 South Sepulveda
(310) 479-2055
Usually has 2 to 3 plays running at
the same time.

Pacific Resident Theater
703 Venice Blvd.
(310) 301-3971
Apprenticeships available.

Santa Monica Civic Center
1855 Main Street, Santa Monica
(310) 458-8551

Santa Monica Playhouse
1211 4th Street
310-394-9779

Shutters on the Beach—(a must for
coffee and desert by their fireplace)
1 Pico Blvd.
(310) 587-1717

Culver City Studios
10202 Washington Blvd.
(310) 244-4000

Theatrical Botanicum
1419 Topanga Canyon
(310) 455-2322
Great Outdoor theater. Accepts pictures and resumes.

Venice Beach Boardwalk
Every weekend on the Ocean Front panhandlers, hipsters, families, artists, celebs, hippies, and exercise nuts. Walk along the Boardwalk and take in the sites.

Venice Canals
SE of Venice Blvd. and Pacific Ave

Vidiots
(The coolest video store in the west, everything you can think of they have it and more)
302 W Pico Blvd. (at Third St.)
(310) 392-8508

VALLEY

Academy of Arts and Sciences
5220 Lankersheim
North Hollywood
(818) 754-2800

Art's Deli
1224 Ventura Blvd., Studio City
(818) 762-1221

CBS Radford Studios
4024 Radford Street
(818) 655-5000

Disney Studios
500 S. Buena Vista Blvd., Studio City
(818) 560-1000

Dreamworks-Amblian Entertainment
100 Universal Plaza, #477
Universal City, CA
(818) 733-7000

Dupars Restaurant
12036 Ventura Blvd., Studio City
(818) 766-4437

Eclectic Café
5156 Lankershim Blvd., Noho
(818) 760-2233

Jerry's Deli (food and bowling!)
12655 Ventura Blvd.
(818) 980-4245

Residuals Bar
11042 Ventura Blvd., Studio City
(818) 761-8301

Samuel French Theater and Film Book Shop
11963 Ventura Blvd. (off Laurel Canyon Blvd.)
(818) 762-0535

Teru Sushi
Ventura Blvd., Studio City
(818) 763-6201
Always packed with soap and TV actors. The sushi is excellent as well!

Universal Studios
100 Universal City, Burbank
(818) 777-1000

Warner Brothers Studios
4000 Warner Blvd., Burbank
(818) 954-6000

VALLEY THEATRES

The Antaeus Company
4916 Vineland Avenue
North Hollywood, CA 91601
(818) 506-5436

Celtic Art Center
4843 Laurel Canyon Blvd.
Studio City, CA
(818) 760-8322
Yearly membership. Gaelic choir.

Colony Theater
555 N. 3rd St.
Burbank, CA
(818) 558-7000

Deaf West
5114 Lankershim Blvd., Noho
(818) 762-2998
All productions are both spoken and signed.

El Portal Center For the Arts
5269 North Lankershim, Noho
(818) 508-4200

Falcon Theater
4252 Riverside Drive, Burbank
(818) 955-8101

Interact Theater Company
5215 Bakman St.
Noho, CA
(818) 765-8732

Laurel Grove Theater
12265 Ventura Blvd., Studio City
(818) 760-8368
Jack Heller-Artistic Director
Susan Peretz-conducts classes

Lonnie Chapman Group Rep Theater
10900 Burbank Blvd., Noho
(818) 769-7529

The Road Theater
5108 Lankershim—N. Hollywood
(818) 761-8838

The Secret Rose
11246 Magnolia Blvd, North Hollywood
(818) 763-4430

Third Stage
2811 W. Magnolia Blvd
Burbank CA
(818) 842-4725

Two Roads Theater
4348 Tujunga Ave.
Studio City, CA 91604
(818) 761-0704

The Victory Theater
3326 West Victory Blvd.
Burbank CA
(818) 843-9253
(818) 841-4404

CHAPTER 3

Month Three, Step Three

Who's Who And What's What:
The Lingo Of
The Entertainment Business

> "Where is the Wagon with all the Honey?"
> Ram Bergman—Independent film producer

RAM BERGMAN

I hardly had any production experience at all when I got a job as a Production Assistant on a movie called "The Prince of Tides." Not only did I have little to zero production experience, I was not completely fluent in the English language. The shoot, I was hired on, was at night and the weather had suddenly dropped from 70 degrees to about 30 degrees.

I am running around in jeans, a tee shirt, and a light leather jacket completely freezing. The union guys saw how cold I was and told me that if I wanted to be in this business, I have to be prepared for anything including sudden weather changes. This is advice coming from guys that have three sets of shoes, just in case! At one point, the second AD says to me over the walkie-talkie radio "Ram, come find me in the Honeywagon."

I had absolutely no idea what a Honeywagon was so I took it really literally…I didn't know…I figured there was some wagon…somewhere…that had honey in it…for what, I had no idea, but what else could it be? So, here I am racing around looking for a wagon that looked like it could store honey. The AD keeps calling me over the walkie-talkie "Where are you? What's wrong with you?" I wasn't responding because I didn't want him to know I had no idea what I was looking for. Finally the AD sees me running around and stops me. "You were supposed to meet me here forty minutes ago. What were you doing?"

That's when I learned what the Honeywagon really is. You can imagine how I felt when the next question over the walkie was "What's your 20?"

When you visit a new country for the first time, it is wise to brush up on your language skills and bring a dictionary, so you understand words that may be unfamiliar. The same is true for Hollywood. There is a whole language that may be foreign to you. This chapter will help you brush up on your lingo and provide you with some common terms, so you will appear fluent and professional even if you are still learning.

COMMON TERMS AND ABBREVIATIONS:

A.D.—Assistant Director—The crewmember who follows out a number of duties for the director, including schedule the shoot days, arrange the logistics, and call the cast and crew and tell them where to meet for the day's filming. He also maintains order on the set and may be there instead of the director for rehearsals. The A.D. gives the order for the camera and sound equipment to begin recording. He's your contact if there is anything that you need, especially if there is something wrong with your pay or hours. Sometimes there may be more than one assistant director working under the A.D.; a 2nd A.D., 3rd A.D., who may be your contact.

Action—After the camera and sound equipment are "rolling" or recording, the director will say "action" and you should begin performing. It's your favorite word! Action is also what the character's do during a scene, their specific movements.

Ad Lib—Making up dialogue and movements as you go even while you have a perfectly good script. Some director's love ad-libing—most writers hate ad-libs.

AEA:—Actors' Equity Association (The union for theater actors)

Agent—A representative for the actor. This person works for the actor to help him obtain work(Agents are hard to get, especially in LA , but read on for helpful tips to for finding and securing an agent representation)

Animation—Mickey Mouse is animation, but so are the dinosaurs from Jurassic Park.

Apple Box—A wooden crate used to raise performers or objects to a desired height for a better shot. Humphrey Bogart used an apple box to stand on because he was so short but didn't want to appear that way on film.

Art Director—The crewmember that makes and sets up all the props needed for the film. If it's a big budget film he gets a new title, Set Designer, and he draws out all the sets with the director. The people underneath him build it and even others put it out to be filmed. On a small, low budget film he might have to design, make, and place it on the set.

Assistant Producer—No one knows what this crewmember really does. He may just be an investor or he might be the lawyer or he may actually be coordinating the filming and handling problems as they arise on set. People in Hollywood like to claim that they're assistant producers.

Audition—The actor's interview. Your chance to show your talent.

Avail—This means you have been asked to a put aside a certain date or dates for a possible booking. This is a hold for a job, not a confirmation.

Back Stage West—The industry trade paper or "rag" that lists auditions and other local info for actors. In NY it's just called the Backstage.

Back Story-The story behind the character. It is where their motivation comes from.

Back To One—This is one of those phrases the A.D. will shout out. It means go back to the first place or "mark" he told you to stand at before the director shouted "action". Basically the director wants to do it again, so hurry up and get ready. (see From the Top)

Bit Player—Small parts with no dialogue

Blocking—Where the director wants you to stand or be while you are speaking your lines. Directors and crew get pissed when you mess up your blocking, so write it down if you can. (see Mark and Back to One)

Boom Operator—This crewmember holds the microphone on a long pole or boom so that it's not in the picture.

Boutique Agency—This is a small talent agency usually only representing, approximately, no more than 50 clients.

Bump—It means a raise in pay and you get a bigger part. This usually happens in commercials, which is how you get speaking part (see Taft Hartley) and into the **Screen Actors Guild** (see S.A.G.). It's a good thing so stop complaining.

Buzz—This is what you've wanted all your acting life, people talking about you and thinking of you.

Call Back—They loved you at the audition so much they want to see you again. Trouble is that there are probably other actors they want to see anyway.

Call Sheet—Ask for and make sure you have one of these sheets of paper. It lists all the crewmembers and actors and what they do on set.

Plus it gives you the time (see Call Time) that you have to be on the next day's location. The 2nd A.D. or production coordinator should have this for you.

Call Time—This is the time when you have to be at a certain location to get ready for your big moment. Don't be late!

Casting Director—The crewmember whose job it is to hire all the actors in the film or commercial production. Try to stay on the good side of this person. But don't go too far and become a casting couch bimbo. If you do you won't be taken seriously.

Clap Board—This is that snapping piece of wood they thrust in and "clap" in every shot to synch up the sound with the picture.

Close Up—This is your shining moment, when the camera solely focuses on your face and you dominate the whole picture. It's the moment your mother can say, "That's my boy!" Sometimes they do an extreme close up on your hands, eyes, or those huge volcano sized pimples.

Commercial Copy—The script you audition with for a commercial.

Commercials—Those thirty or sixty-second little movies between the episodes of your favorite sit-com or drama. Hint: they pay the most money.

Continuity—The crewmember that is in charge of making sure that everything in the same scene matches from one shot to the next so that it looks like it was all done at the same time.

Contract—This piece of paper makes sure you can take the producers to court if they fail to pay you or live up to what you and the production company agreed. Save it if you have one, get one if you don't.

Costume Designer—This crewmember designs and probably makes many of the dresses, shirts, and uniforms, etc. everyone wears in front of the camera.

Craft Services—Beware. There are tables full of goodies like M&M's, cheese and crackers, peanuts, and other delectably scrumptious food and drinks that will make you fat and bloated if you don't be careful. I recommend asking for healthier food and most likely they will have some. But its good knowing that you can eat all the snacks you want.

Crane Shot—It's when they use a construction crane gizmo to lift the camera far or high away and then move it around. It may start out as an extremely wide shot and end with a close-up. There are special crane operators who usually work these mechanical marvels, you'll have to trust that they know what they're doing.

Credits—It's when your name is lit up on the big screen. It proves that it was you who played that part so well.

Cross—It's a term used by the A.D. It means pass in front of the camera. Usually it's said to a throng of extras. The director often needs these to reveal a scene or change to another scene.

Cue Cards—Pieces of card board that have the couple of lines you need to say. Everybody uses them, although you should try to memorize them. But if you didn't, just ask for these just to be safe.

Cue—The word or action by a fellow actor which tells you to start acting.

Cut—When the A.D. or director yells this out, it means stop. There is usually something wrong that needs to be fixed or the scene is over. (see Back to One and Print)

Cutting Room Floor—You don't want to end up here. It's the killing floor where your image and voice go to die. Forget about credit, cry for a bit, and then hit the pavement cause it's better to have loved and lost then never to have loved at all.

D.P.—(a.k.a. Director of Photographer or Cinematographer) This crewmember is responsible for every lighting nuance and subtly. He can make you look beautiful or nasty. Try to bribe him, but it usually doesn't work. Ask him for some beauty light and he'll laugh at you. He's a hard working professional.

Dailies—The film that was shot the previous day. It's been processed and can now be viewed by the director and producers and anyone else concerned to see if they can move on to today's events.

Deal Memo—This is a letter stating the days you will be working and the amount you will be paid!!

Director—The person you most want to hire you; the creative boss and vision behind the project. He helps the actor to bring the character to life.

Dolly Shot—A sheep gets killed by a bullet? Maybe in Bulgaria. But in Hollywood it's where they put the camera on a fancy contraption so it doesn't shake while they roll it across a set of tracks.

Down Stage—The space closest to the camera or audience. It is a stage direction. (see Up Stage and then say "duh, of course.)

Dubbing—The recording of sound to an image that's already been shot. It can be for background, sound foreign languages or strange, gurgling noises. There are some funny directors out there in Hollywood.

Editor—This crewmember hides in a dark room with a computer and puts all the dailies or shots together in a movie. He and the director drink cappuccinos all evening.

Establishing Shot—The opening shot of a scene that establishes location, mood, and gives the general lowdown on what the scene is all about.

Executive Producer—This person is the cappo-di-tutti capo, the big boss man. He owns and runs the whole production. Tell him to move and you're fired quicker than an ant under a magnifying glass.

Extras—Actors hired to fill the background of a scene. As a newcomer, it might be fun to do it once to get to be on a set; but you don't want to get known as an extra. There is a stigma about working in this capacity.

Fade In—Going from dark to light. On a stage, the lights go on and the play's underway. In a film, the editor makes a fade in; so don't sweat it.

Fade Out—going from light to dark. On a stage, the lights go off and the play's in between acts or is over. Or you've had too many drinks and like Porky Pig says, "T-T-T-that's all folks!"

Featured Extra—Where you have no lines but your face is in the shot. In other words you could tell your grandma in Wichita that she can see you on the big screen, but just for a second.

First Team—The lead actors.

First Unit—The principle crew, the people who do most of the work.

Fitting—Your appointment, either before or during the shoot, when you get to try on lots of costumes and have them custom fitted for you to wear on stage or set. Don't be late. It's also when you realize those M&M's at the craft service table are doing you wrong. (see Costume Designer or Stylist)

Flashback—While it is also a strange side effect of LSD, it's when a shot or scene has taken place in the past before the present time established in the film. Trippy.

Frame—The borders of the image on the screen that enclose the pictures like a frame on your great-grandmother's painting. Be sure to stay in the frame for as long as possible.

From The Top—The A.D. shouts this out and you have to do it all again from the very beginning. (see Go Back to One)

Gaffer—This crewmember and his helpers (see Grips) set up lights for the Cinematographer (see D.P.).

Go See—Similar to an audition, the time when you get seen by the casting person. It's a term more frequently used with models.

Grips—This crewmember is usually a big burly man with lots of tools putting together all the rigs, lights, and facades.

Hair Stylist—This crewmember does your hair the way the director wants it. Ask them to be gentle to your lovely locks.

Honey Wagon—Read Ram's little ditty at the beginning of this chapter and don't jump ahead. Hint: It's a fancy name for a truck with a toilet and the make-up department.

Key Light—This is the main lamp that gives you that special glow.

Line Readings—You don't want to be accused of this, because it means you're delivering the line in a fixed and stilted way. Get to those emotions.

Location Scout—This crewmember finds the location for the shoot.

Location—The place away from the studio where the cameras are going to be to take your picture. Better get there and don't be late.

Looping—The process of re-recording dialogue over the movie as it's playing. (see Dubbing)

Make-up Artist—This crewmember applies cosmetics to your delicate eyes, lips, and proboscis. Hope that they have steady hands and don't have a hangover. If they're applying prosthetics or heavy amounts of latex to make you look like a dog, they prefer to be called Special Effects Make—Up Artist.

Manager—This person acts as a liaison between you, the actor, and the agent. They help shape your career. They act like your Den mother and guide you on dress, work decisions, and money matters. At different levels, the manager will work in different capacities.

Mark—In a film or commercial, its one or more places where the AD or Director tells you to stand. It's your order of blocking. (see Blocking and Back to One)

Monologue—(a.k.a. Soliloquy) A complete speech or reading given by an actor.

MOS—This German director would say "Mit Out Sound", he meant "without sound". It means you can talk at the craft service table or snore, because it's just the camera recording not the microphones.

Motivation—The reason behind why you are saying the words on the paper the way only you can say them. (see Back Story)

On Camera Class—A class in which you learn how to relate to the camera. They record what you are doing so you can see yourself over and over again. It's almost like the real thing, except that you could mess up and not get fired.

On Hold—When the AD, agent, or production coordinator tells you that you shouldn't make any other plans for a certain day(s) except to be at location. (see Unveil)

Off Screen—If you are off screen then you aren't in the picture. Whoops! Better learn your marks. (see Frame)

P.A.—It means Production Assistant. This crewmember is usually young, doesn't know much, and working his way up the ladder. Don't pick on him, because they may be the next Speilberg or Coppala. Sometimes they're college students trying to pay for their way through school, film school. Get it?

Pick It Up—When a director shouts this, it means increase the pace of the scene.

P.O.V.—(Point of View) When the camera pretends to be one of the characters.

Print—On a film, the director says this to the camera crew when he gets exactly what he wants. It comes from printing or processing the film (see Cut and Dailies)

Producer—This crewmember knows and gets everything that's needed for the shoot or production. Know him and you'll get some work definitely. Of course, don't be naive. A lot of people claim to be producers, but they've never even seen a shoot. Warning: producers will do anything to get what they want.

Production Designer—(see Art Director)

Production Manager—The crewmember who is responsible for all the shoot's daily business, i.e. bookkeeping and crew information. Smart as a whip, they can usually spot trouble and a weakness like an eagle can spot a salmon under some rough surf.

Property Master—The crewmember who is in charge of all the props. (see Art Director)

Props—A gun or a pen is a prop. A car can be a prop. Anything that is used on a set or stage is a prop.

Red Light—If you see a red light go on, stop moving! The cameras and sound are rolling, we are filming, don't open the door or make any noise. (see Sound Stage)

Role—The part you are cast in silly.

Rolling—Cameramen and sound recordists say this to the AD to tell him that they are recording. (see Action and Cut)

Ross Report—The little book that lists all the agents, soaps and shows being filmed.

SAG (Screen Actors Guild)—This is the union for those who want to make it to the big time. (see Taft-Hartley)

Scene—This is a segment of the script. Usually for TV and soap auditions you are asked to read a scene.

Screen Play—(Teleplay) A feature film length script. If it looks like a duck, quacks like a duck, it must be a duck.

Script Supervisor—(see Continuity)

Script—A whole bunch of writers sit in front of computers making characters and having them talk. It's all done with words and magic.

Set Decorator—(see Art Director)

Shooting Schedule—This is the order and arrangement of the film or commercial to be photographed. It changes day to day, so keep on top of it. (see Call Sheet)

Side—Small versions of the script or scene that you can use while rehearsing.

Sign In Sheet—This is a tracking of every one who is to audition that day. You sign it when you walk in and are called in to the room from that order, like a reservation list at a restaurant.

Silent Bit—An important part that requires no talking.

Slate—(see Clapboard)

Sound Stage—This is where you film when you are not on location. It usually looks like a huge warehouse or airplane hanger. There are big doors and padding on the walls. (see Red Light)

Special Effects—Boom! Crash! The explosions, the car accidents, everything that makes it look like something extraordinary happened when in reality it was done either on a computer or in a sound stage.

Speed—Not the movie. The cameraman and the sound recordist say this back to the AD when their instruments have reached the proper speed to record properly.

Spokesperson—An actor, model or celebrity hired to promote and represent a product. Think of Catherine Zeta Jones representing T-Mobile.

Spot—More than a dog's name. It's the name of the segment or commercial being filmed.

Stand-Ins—These people stand in for the actors when they are lighting a scene. They relieve the main actors from standing there all day in under the hot lights.

Still Photographer—The person who shoots still pictures on a set for either publicity or continuity. They may also do headshots, so go ask them for their portfolio.

Stock Footage—Historical or archival film from libraries, museums, or stock footage houses.

Story Board—A frame-by-frame drawing and breakdown of the action of the script. The director uses it to plan out his shots before it costs a million a day.

Stunt Person—The crewmember who gets paid to take the fall off a building or get burned alive.

Suits—Studio or TV executives.

Taft Hartley—An upgrade from an extra part, which gives you the chance to get into the Screen Actors Guild. (see SAG)

Take—When shooting a commercial or film, each scene might take several tries or takes.

Talking Head—Derogatory for a spokesperson

TBA—On the call sheet or any schedule you might see these three letters. They mean "To Be Announced". Sometimes a production coordinator likes to get tricky and use TBD or "To Be Decided". (see Call Sheet)

Teleplay—(see Screenplay)

Track—The sound. Some things are just simple.

Trades—Industry papers (See *Variety* and *Back Stage West*)

Turn Around Time—You may get to sleep at 4 am on a shoot. The turn around time is the amount of time you have to sleep before you have to be back on the set. Sometimes the turn around sucks and you have only 4 hours to sleep. Most times, you have 8 hours to zonk out.

Under Five—Speaking part, where you have less than five lines. A different contract than a principle, a step above an extra. If you get bumped from an extra, an *Under Five* can get you Taft Hartleyed.

Unit Manager—(see Production Manager)

Upstage—The farthest area from the camera or the audience. (see Down stage)

V/O—(voice over). It's when they put your voice or song over the moving picture. (see Dub)

Waiver—Someone at sometime is going to ask you to sign a waiver. It may mean there are going to be residuals or more money in it for you. But what a waiver really means is that you are waiving your rights to or about something. Don't do this until your agent tells you it's okay.

Don't be bullied by people in the production. It's a legal contract and your agent should be aware of anything you are going to sign.

Walk Around—When the spokes person walks around the product.

Wild Line—A line of dialogue wasn't clear so they'll have record it without the cameras and add it to the scene in the editing.

What's Your 20—You'll hear this a lot on the walkie-talkies everyone on the set is wearing. It means, where the hell are you.

Wrap—The end of the shoot when the crew and cast are done working. The "martini shot" is when the very last shot is being taken. When it's done and the AD shouts "Wrap" then everyone cheers and starts to break out the six packs.

These definitions are just a brief overview of the terms you should come to be familiar with. The film and TV world are full of strange vocabulary. Eventually all of these terms will be second nature to you. So head to the craft service in your kitchen call it a wrap and take a long turn around, 'cause tomorrow is going to be a busy day.

Now that you are acquainted with the jargon, let's put your craft to work. That way you can test that newfound lingo you just acquired. Chapter 4 will emphasize the importance of classes as part of your new life in LA.

CHAPTER 4

Month Four: Step Four

Classes, Classes, Classes

> "Classes are more than perfecting a craft; they're about friendship, laughter, tears, healing, acceptance, reality learning and love, both of self and others"
>
> April Jayne—Sitcom Actress

Regardless of the number of credits you have on your résumé, there is only one bottom line—you have a responsibility, with or without representation, to create, expand and promote yourself. This is imperative for your career. Beginning actors, working actors, even established name actors all share the same desire to work, increase their sphere of influence, and improve their creative and financial value within the entertainment industry.

Rob Bowman, director and producer of the *X Files* television series and movie states, "There is never any rest for the weary. Every phase of an actor's career presents obstacles that need to be confronted and overcome." Your career has to be the most important aspect of your life. This may mean sacrifice and tough decisions. However, if you want to attain success, your career should supersede anything else in your life. This means immersing yourself in your art. Becoming a member of the acting community means giving up the luxury of ever being complacent or lazy, regardless of your professional stature.

So how do I get there? What do I do to start? Where do I develop the relationships and contacts I keep hearing people say I should have? CLASSES, CLASSES, CLASSES!!

I cannot emphasize enough the importance of being in classes. Classes are where you learn to hone a specific technique. It's the arena in which an actor begins to establish relationships with their peers and the entertainment community. Here you will meet people who will remain in your acting life and beyond as friends, colleagues, mentors, and even competitors.

These initial relationships with other actors will be the beginning of your professional networking pool. Your fellow thespians will understand, sympathize and motivate you because you are fighting the same battles, trying to win the same war, and dealing with similar struggles and obstacles. Moreover, these new relationships will remain true if you stay true to yourself and your dream. An actor's life is a constant emotional roller coaster and a class will offer you a large dose of consistency and support. You will find that it will be your artistic anchor. However, that is not enough; also try to create a lot of balances in all the other areas of your life. Every bit of constancy is essential for staying sane and focused in this nutty business.

Dori

If you are one of the few actors who is naturally brilliant and is hired because of your immense raw talent and instinct, then learning some form of a technique can be discovered on the job. For the rest of us who have to work at it and learn how to use our talent and even discover the immense abilities we have hidden, class is essential.

As a former acting teacher and a working manager, I must stress the importance of being in a good acting class with a good teacher. This is something I require from all my clients. An inspiring acting teacher will double as a *mentor* and a role model. The acting teacher will be someone you can trust and believe in—a person who has insight and ability to open you up emotionally and help you find your talent.

This person, your mentor, shows you what is possible. They will push, prod, cajole, and even embarrass you a little, to move you up to the next level because they know that overcoming your obstacles will lead to work. This remains true even for professional actors who work time and time again. They, too, need a guide, a coach, and a director who understands their strengths and respects their talents. Therefore, trust between the teacher and actor must be essential in order to insure a student's success not just in the class, but out in the professional world.

For me, this mentor was Milton Katselas. Declaring myself a member of his class made me feel a part of something greater than myself. As a newcomer to LA, this class became my grounding, my community, and the method/school of acting I choose to study. I studied Milton's technique as religiously as one would study the Bible.

During the time I spent studying and then teaching acting under Milton, I truly understood how a person needs incredible perseverance as well as an understanding of the business in order to become a working actor. I experienced first hand that class, in its best form was, as Milton said "…a microcosm of the industry." I learned that class was neither a sanctuary nor a retreat from the daily grind of being an actor. It was not a place, no matter how hard I wanted it to be, where I could find solitude and hide from the task at hand—

acting, getting work, having a career. Milton's acting class was the arena in which I learned to orchestrate myself, where I discovered how to create order and structure, and success. I chose Milton's method because I loved what he had to say and how he said it. I continue to be amazed at how cleverly Milton molded his personality and his critiques according to the temperament of his students. I could wax on about Milton forever, but that is the way you should be with the teacher you find.

My experience and devotion to Milton's class is not unique. Just look at the Academy Awards to see how many actors thank their teachers for believing in and inspiring them. Many working actors praise and cheer whatever disciple they've been taught. This is why it is imperative to choose your instructor with great care and confidence. What works for one person may not work for another. Some actors prefer warm emotional nurturing teachers while other actors may prefer a more nuts and bolts, get right to the point, kind of teacher. You need to identify the right teacher for you, the right chemistry for your particular temperament.

A good teacher establishes a class that provides you with the space and opportunity to workout and stretch your acting limbs over and over again like a good gym. It gives you, the actor, a discipline and forces you to take responsibility for your career by working on scenes, monologues, and cold readings. You are obligated to work, work, work until you break through the emotional obstacles that hinder you from experiencing a new level of work and artistry.

However, in order to be a successful actor, it can't just be all acting and art. It's also means knowing how to set aside enough hours in the day to hit the phones and the pavement for acting work. This is another aspect of classes. It's a world that should offer you more than just a technique or method. It should provide concrete advice on the business, in regards to pictures, resumes, showcases, and other ways the actor needs to market themselves.

I learned through class, and employ it now as a manager, that being a one or two trick pony gets you only so far in this business. Getting the immediate job, series, or even the three-picture deal is not the end, especially if you don't have the ability to constantly produce the goods. Think ahead, not one or two years, but rather five and ten. Have a plan. Discipline and good business head will present you with an advantage.

In contrast to other creative artists such as dancers or musicians, the actor is normally the least disciplined. It usually never occurs to actors that the road to becoming a professional includes developing and maintaining a daily routine, which means working on scenes, monologues, cold readings, as well as, voice and body work. The lines you rehearse over and over again (*ad infinitum, ad nauseum*), the repetition of reading material cold, and the other emotional exercises in your routine strengthen your creative instrument. Focus and training are two attributes that do not appear out of thin air. They are elements that ultimately define you as a professional, but are born out of a desire to learn a specific style and approach to the business. A strong, well rounded focused actor sells. If you are new to the business and meeting with managers, agents, and casting directors for the first time, they want to see that you take your craft, the business, and them seriously.

All in all, a beginner or a professional needs to constantly work at acting and the business of acting. Classes encourage you to keep in artistic shape, especially when you aren't being paid, don't have to be on the film set, or in rehearsal. It's a place where after you finish working for a few months, a year, two years or even more, that you can return to and discover something exciting which will propel you even further.

Eventually, you will find and tune your creative instrument. Your approach may be a piece-meal combination of several different "methods" or ideas. Acting is a life-long process. If you decide to stay in it for the long haul or if you ditch acting altogether, the skills you acquire in your acting classes will have crossover benefits into many other areas of your life. They should help you identify your strengths and weaknesses as well as enlighten new areas.

If class doesn't make you think, question, and challenge, it's probably not the right class unless you're there just to make new friends and get dates.

Practical Tips For Choosing A Class

There are many different personal variables to take into account when looking for a class:

- *Never choose a class because other people say it's the best in town or the most popular. Trust your instincts and do a lot of research.*
- *Ask if you can audit a class (sit in the class for free).*
- *Set up an interview with the teacher.*
- *Find out who are some of the alumni of the class or school and are they working. Try to talk to some students.*
- *Make sure you can afford the price and time commitment.*
- *Ask agents or other professionals (not actors) if they know of the teacher or school.*
- *Use some good judgment; don't be impatient and over eager. In other words, don't get sold by someone who is out to get your money.*

There will be a lot of sales pressure, but only commit if *you* are confident and like the teacher and other students. Don't act like some country bumpkin and follow along blindly. And if in the first couple of classes don't feel right, don't feel bullied into staying. Keep investigating until the match feels right. Classes are expensive—so invest wisely.

Acting, Voice, and Audition Classes

These are some of the more popular and established acting classes in LA. However, there are many, many more than those listed here, which are possibly just as good. There may even be a class not listed which would work better for you. This selection is just a starting point, similar to finding your favorite hangout. It is all personal taste!!

> Note: Some teachers do not list their addresses, because they do not encourage drop-ins. Please call to schedule an appointment.

Acting Schools and Private Teachers

American Academy of Dramatic Arts
1336 North La Brea Blvd.
Hollywood, CA
(323) 464-2777
A two year program.

Actor's Workout Studio
4735 Lankershim
North Hollywood, CA
(818) 506-3903

Actors Studio
Only for members—a place where professional actors work out. Must audition. *Call for audition schedule*
8341 DeLongpre
West Hollywood, CA
(323) 654-7125

Stella Adler
6773 Hollywood Blvd.
Hollywood, CA 90028
(323) 465-4446
(323) 465-4464
Accomplished actors teach master classes.

William Alderson Acting Studio
(323) 852-1816
(323) 669-1534

821 ¾ Fairfax Ave.
W. Hollywood, CA
Meisner Technique

Joel Asher Studio
(818) 785-1551
13448 Albers Ave.
ShermanOaks, CA

Joanne Barron & D.W. Brown Studio
320 Willshire Blvd.
Santa Monica, CA
(310) 451-3311

Beverly Hills Playhouse
(310) 855-1556
Milton Katseles
254 S. Robertson Dr.
Beverly Hills, CA

City College Theater Dept.
855 North Vermont Ave.—LA
(323) 953-4000 ex 2990
See—Beth Hogan—also associated with the Odyssey Theatre.
Intermediate and advanced classes—inexpensive

Darryl Hickman's Acting Workshop
(818) 344-5796

Alan Miller
(818) 907-6262

Larry Moss Studio
2437 Main Street, Santa Monica
(310) 829-9692
Private coach to many stars.

Playhouse West School of Repertory Theater
4250 Lankershim
North Hollywood, CA
(818) 881-6520
Meisner Technique

Joe Salazar
(323) 882-6433

Santa Monica Playhouse
1211 4th Street
Santa Monica, CA 90401
(310) 394-9779

The Lee Strasberg Theater Institute
7936 Santa Monica Blvd.
LA CA 90046
(323) 650-7777
Guest speakers and special events

Theater of Arts
1621 N. McCadden Pl.
West Hollywood, CA
(323) 463-2500
Oldest acting school on West Coast; theater and on-camera classes.

University of California
UCLA extension/entertainment studies
10995 Le Conte, Westwood
(310) 825-9064
Courses and workshops taught by industry professionals.

Third Street Theater
8142 West Third Street
(323) 852-0614
Susan Peretz—accomplished actress and teacher

Victory Theater
3326 West Victory Blvd., Burbank, 91505
(818) 843-9253
Maria Golbetti—Actress, Director, Producer, Teacher

Comedy and Improv

Comedy Store
8433 W.Sunset Blvd.
West Hollywood, CA 90046
(323) 656-6225
Open mike Sunday and Monday

Groundlings School
8307 Melrose Ave
LA CA 90046
(213) 934-4747

Ice House Comedy Clinic
(626) 577-1894
24 N. Mentor
Pasadena, CA
Open auditions the 24th of each month.

Improv Academy
8162 Melrose Ave
LA CA 90046
(323) 651-2583

LA Connection Comedy
Theater
13442 Ventura Blvd.
Sherman Oaks, CA 91423
(818) 710-1320
Open auditions on Wednesday

The Harvey Lembeck Comedy
Workshop
(310) 271-2831

Second City
Training Center and Studio
8156 Melrose Avenue
LA, CA 90046
(323) 658-8190

On Camera Commercial Technique

American Film Institute
2021 N. Western Ave.
Warner Bldg., Rm. 105
LA CA 90027
(323) 856-7600

Film Acting For The
Professional/David Kagen
(818) 752-9678

Tepper/Gallegos, Inc.
(Commercial Classes)
639 North Larchmont Blvd., #207
LA, CA
(323) 469-3577
Agent showcases

TVI Actors Studio
14429 Ventura Blvd.
Sherman Oaks, CA 91423
(818) 784-6500
Cold reading and on camera classes
given by casting directors—beginners and advanced

Weist Barron Hill Acting for
Television and Film
4300 W. Magnolia Blvd.
Burbank, CA 91505
(818) 846-5595

Voice Coaching
—Speech and Dialects—

Mark Anton
2217 West Olive, Burbank
(818) 955-9535
Very Nurturing. Great with
non-singers.

Howard Austin
(818) 895-7464
Vocal training and coaching

Bill Dearth
1326 Magnolia Blvd.
NoHo, CA
(818) 761-1051
Excellent for dialects.

Robert Easton
"the dialect doctor"
(818) 985-2222

The Steven Memel Studio
4760 Halbrent
Sherman Oaks
(818) 789-0474
Vocal technique-geared to performance

Larry Moss
Santa Monica
(310) 395-4284
Excellent for dialects and diction

Seth Riggs
(323) 938-4780
Excellent for singing auditions, but expensive; he can also refer you to his assistants if he is too expensive

Susan Streitwiesser, MA
(323) 655-6669
Singing

Marjory Taylor, Ph.D., Ed.D.
West Hollywood
(310) 246-1743
Singing, coaching and accents

Mark Vogel
18644 Sherman Way
Reseda 91335
(818) 881-3651
Coaching for singing auditions

Carol Weiss Studio
Hollywood
(323) 460-6006
Coach for musical theater auditions

Dance Classes and Studios

Anna Cheselka
12445 Moorpark, Studio City
(818) 769-0566
Ballet

Madeline Clark Dance Studios
10852 Burbank Blvd.
North Hollywood
(818) 359-2007 (studio)
(818) 506-7763
equity auditions often held

The Edge
1020 North Cole, 4th Fl.,
Hollywood, (323) 962-7733
The hottest place in town right now—you will see many recognizable actors

Hama's Dance Center
1217 Moorpark, Studio City
(818) 985-8701

Landis Dance
5113 Lankershim, North Hollywood
(818) 753-5081

Debbie Reynolds Studios
6514 Lankershim Ave.
North Hollywood 91606
(818) 985-3193
Dance auditions here

Kristin Sauter—Private teacher
(818) 590-8039
Excellent at teaching actors & singers to dance quickly (reasonable prices)

Patsy Swayze's Dancers Studio
1788 East Los Angeles Blvd.
Simi Valley
(805) 583-3216
Great dance studio, run by Patrick Swayze's mother

Twenty Questions You Need To Ask
Before You Sign Up For Classes

❑   Is it an on-camera class?

❑   Is it a scene study class?

❑   Can you audit the class before signing up?

❑   Is it an ongoing program?

❑   What is the reputation of the teacher?

❑   What is the level of experience of the other students?

❑   Does the school do showcases?

❑   Are any of the students currently working?

❑   Who are some of their alumni?

❑   Is there a specific technique they are married to, i.e. Meisner, Strasberg

❑   Does the class help students learn about the business, as well as the craft?

❑   How many students per class?

❑   Do you get to work every class?

❑   Does the class help you find audition material?

❑   How does the instructor determine what class you are going to be in?

❑   Can you bring in audition material to work on in class?

❑   How many times a week does the class meet?

❑   Is it expected that students get together and rehearse outside of class?

❑   Does the class incorporate any movement or voice work?

❑   Are all the students committed to a professional career?

Only commit if you are confident and like the teacher and other students. Don't believe the hype.

Classes I Audited this Month

School	Teacher
Phone	Days
Price	
Comments	

School	Teacher
Phone	Days
Price	
Comments	

School	Teacher
Phone	Days
Price	
Comments	

School	Teacher
Phone	Days
Price	
Comments	

School	Teacher
Phone	Days
Price	
Comments	

Lead with your heart and watch your wallet with your brain

CHAPTER 5

Step Five, Month Five

Inventing yourself

> **INVENTION**—noun. (1) The conception of an idea (2) The exercise of creative or imaginative power in art (3) The power or faculty of inventing, devising, or originating (4) The process of choosing ideas appropriate to the subject.

DORI

The importance of creating yourself, creating a "look" that is memorable and unique, does not mean going away from who you are. It means highlighting your personal, physical and emotional attributes, and in the right combination, it can make the statement, "This is who I am; this is what I'm about." It requires an understanding of fashion, hairstyles, and make-up. All of these elements affect people's perception about you. They constitute the marketing of your image. For instance, a man with a rough looking beard, wearing a leather jacket and bandanna would be marketing himself as a biker or rough-neck. He may be a teddy bear, but his look sells him as a biker. Or take a woman with big hair, lots of make-up and cleavage. She's looking for a part as a stripper or hooker.

The invention process, inventing yourself as an actor, also involves understanding your casting and the roles you are right for. The people hiring you—casting directors, producers and directors—will want to see a person, not just an actor. When they look at your headshot or meet you for the first time, they need to get an immediate feeling about who you are as well as what you have to convey and the parts you might be right for.

Headshots play an important part in this invention process. It is your calling card. It is what casting directors, agents, or anyone involved with hiring sees first. Robert Zuckerman, a well-known industry photographer who has shot such celebrities as Cameron Diaz, David Bowie, Mia Kershner, Ben Stiller, Samuel L. Jackson, Brandon Lee, Christian Slater and Patricia Arquette, has explained, "The photographer cannot create something that is not there. Like a director, he can only help the actor express his own natural beauty, emotions and rawness..." This is *your talent*, the aspects and qualities of your personality that are special and unique to you. These are the elements of yourself that you must learn to develop and convey to help get you the job.

People become actors for a number of reasons. They need to communicate and express who they are and what they feel. Others look at acting as an escape from themselves and their own feelings. The truth is, acting has everything to do with who you are.

A painter uses a number of different tools and materials, such as paints and brushes, to help him manifest his feelings on canvas. The actor's tools are his experiences, feelings and point of view; and, in the process, the actor becomes the canvas. The paintings the actor creates are the characters he plays on stage and/or screen. In the process, creating a character becomes an opportunity for the actor to express himself, thereby revealing a part of who he is as a person and an artist.

For a young actor, defining yourself or learning who you are can be a very daunting experience. There always appears to be more questions than answers. But you need to have an understanding of yourself, your feelings, and your particular point of view. With that comes an understanding of the parts you might be cast in, otherwise known as your **casting** or **castability**. Begin thinking of the roles you are suited for right now. What are the jobs that will get me working and paid as an actor?

Sometimes how we may see ourselves is not always how casting directors and agents see us. The roles we want to be cast in or work on in class may not always be the roles that will help generate our professional career. The purpose of a good acting class is twofold. First, the class will help you learn a useable technique—an approach to the work and art of acting. Here you will be asked to do exercises that open you up emotionally, making you more sensitive and vulnerable to your feelings—be it anger, tears laughter or joy. You will also work on roles from plays and films that may be out of your casting, but they are part of an overall training that will help you develop the tools and creativity you need as an actor.

The second goal of a professional class should be in teaching the actor about his casting. This is not an area that every acting teacher explores or even understands. However it was a concept taught to me by my former acting coach, Milton Katselas. Part of his belief as a director and teacher is that the aim of an acting studio is to get everyone working as professional actors. He is not interested in creating perpetual students. He wants his actors to learn their craft, learn their casting, and carry that with them onto the set and into the professional world.

You must learn to discover the roles you are right for—**your casting**. We can't all be the romantic lead even though there is a romantic leading man or woman in each of us. Discover where you fit in and the roles that are right for you. Recognizing what they are will determine your success as an actor in LA.

You will constantly be asked over and over again, how do you see yourself? What roles do you see yourself playing? What actors do you relate to, where you can say

"That's my part. I can play that role in that film." Do you see yourself as a young Robert Duvall in the 1971 film, *The Godfather*, or in one of his more contemporary films like *The Apostle*? Do you see yourself as a sexy leading man like a young Warren Beatty from the film *Shampoo*, where he played a hair stylist in Beverly Hills who has affairs with all his female clients? The same is obviously true for a woman. Are you a Tia Leoni type—a sophisticated, elegant, beautiful young woman who is a little quirky, but has wonderful comedic abilities? Or, are you more inclined to be cast in parts that have a darker edge and bite? These are some of the questions you have to ask yourself. Think about what roles you can do now, not always what you would love to play. Although hopefully they will overlap, and the parts you love are the parts you play. I have seen and heard of acting careers that have taken off once an actor has understood this concept of casting. This theory came to life for me as I watched even well known actors perfect their roles in class. During the time I studied with Milton, I was fortunate to have been in class with a number of successful working actors such as Tony Danza, Mary Lou Henner, and Alec Baldwin among others.

However, it was Tom Selleck who exemplifies this idea of castability. It was only after he began working in class on leading man roles, those parts originated by such actors as Clark Gable, Gary Cooper, and Cary Grant, did his career really take off. He was already working and well known for his commercials, but the work Milton did with Tom on his castability focused his talents and clarified how he was perceived by others who did the hiring. It was only a short time later that he was hired for the role of Magnum in the television series, *Magnum, P.I.*

Another example of this was related to me once by my old friend Nancy Cartwright, an accomplished actress in her own right who's the voice of Bart Simpson on the animated show, *The Simpsons*. She had originally been called into read for a number of other roles on the show and was prepared to do just that. However, at the audition, she asked the producers if she could read for the role of Bart. Naturally, she told them she would do the other roles, but felt she had a handle on Bart's character and wanted a shot. Nancy knew that in some way Bart was her casting. She understood the concept of casting and within the perimeters of the project was able to deliver the goods and convince them she was Bart. She succeeded and has been doing the role ever since the show first aired.

In the end, it doesn't matter if you read for *The Simpsons* or an epic love story starring Tom Cruise. Your casting, your ability to look at yourself and see the roles that you fit, are the most important lessons you will ever learn.

Working as a professional actor is about getting work, not just studying and trying to perfect every role. Understand that, at this moment, it may only be the one role which gets you working. If it is, do that role over and over again. Do it better and funnier and more personal than anyone else. We are not saying this to limit your ability or to deflate your dreams of becoming the consummate actor. We want you to work. The first role can be the stepping stone to a long and successful career. Take that one part or two that you are great at, then expand your casting. Don't stop, however, doing the very thing that has moved your career forward.

In addition, when you are starting out, do not interfere with the progress of your career by refusing to consider parts you feel may show you in an unfavorable light. An example of this can be seen with actresses who sometimes do not want to play prostitutes. They are afraid they will be type cast and stifle their career and then only be cast in roles that are of that specific nature. It seems ironic that both Elizabeth Shue and Mira Sorvino received Academy acclaim for their breathtaking performances as prostitutes.

Not everyone needs to be Lawrence Olivier or Marlon Brando. We all aspire to achieve great levels in our work, but not everyone is going to attain such brilliance and emotional range. However, that does not mean you cannot be a successful working actor. Nowhere is it written in the acting Bible that an actor has to play a multitude of different roles in order to be considered a great actor. Sometimes an actor is given an opportunity to play the one role that becomes their defining moment. In the case of Jack Nicholson, this role was his brilliant portrayal of McMurphy in *One Flew Over the Cuckoo's Nest,* which earned him an Academy Award for Best Actor. He already had a great deal of success from his other films, such as *Easy Rider* and *Five Easy Pieces,* but the role of McMurphy defined his career. It catapulted him to a new level, a star level where he is considered one of this country's greatest living actors. We see his work and recognize parts of his personality in the people he portrays. He molds a part of himself into each and every character. He never disguises or hides who he is. He brings 'Jack' to the role, whether it is a dramatic part in the thriller *The Shining,* a contemporary historical character like *Hoffa,* or a romantic comedy like *As Good As It Gets.*

The same holds true for Clint Eastwood, an Academy Award winning actor, director, and producer. He built a successful acting career portraying tough and rugged loners. His characters were outsiders who, if need be, would kill another human being. However, they were characters whose actions were based on a strong moral and ethical belief in right and wrong. Clint has also distinguished himself from other actors by bringing his own personal characteristics, physical behavior, and distinctive speech pattern to his characters. This can be seen in his early films such as: *The Good, The Bad and The Ugly,* and *Dirty Harry.* These traits have also translated to his work in more contemporary films like: *In The Line of Fire; Unforgiven; and The Bridges of Madison Country.* In each instance, Clint Eastwood was ostensibly Clint Eastwood. However, based on one character, he created an amazingly successful career that has now made him one of the most influential artists in the entertainment industry. His ability to draw audiences into the theater has given him the opportunity to do work that expands his range . He understands who he is and how to present himself. He knows he wouldn't do Nicholson's role in *The Shining* because it's not his casting.

The same is true of other actors like Shirley McLaine, Goldie Hawn, Diane Keaton, Woody Allen, Al Pacino, Jack Lemmon, Jim Carey or Gwyneth Paltrow. The parts they play are an extension of who they are. The roles they bring to life on either stage or screen are written and rewritten to fit who they are as people and artists. They highlight, as well as enhance, their ability and strength as actors. Al Pacino wants the parts he plays to be written in such a way so as to take advantage of who he is, in addition to his strengths as an actor. That is why Jim Carey, at this point in his career, might not be considered for a dramatic film like *Donny Brasco,* which starred Pacino and Johnny Depp, because it's not his casting and doesn't exploit his strengths as an actor. On the other hand, Jim Carey probably has the emotional depth to be considered a wonderful dramatic actor. If given the right vehicle, he could show his dramatic side. *The Truman Show* was probably the first leg of his journey toward that serious role. Until then, films such as *Mask* and *Liar, Liar* were perfect because they took full advantage of his extraordinary comic abilities.

The concept of casting and the roles actors do or are known for do not detract from who they may be as people. It certainly doesn't minimize or take anything away from them as successful working actors. As an actor, you need to learn how to train your thoughts and view everything with a discerning eye. Your ability to break down a performance and film from one moment to the next is imperative. If you were a visual arts major, you would study every detail of a painter's work, from his brush strokes to the type of paint he uses. You would analyze the minutest details that went into the painting in order to gain a better understanding about the artist and that particular piece of work.

The same is true of any profession—from making shoes to being a clothing designer, to selling stocks and bonds. An actor's business is similar. You need to study in detail the performances of great, well known actors, in addition to the actors whose roles were smaller, but are people you see all the time. You may not remember their names, but you should study their technique, their style, and their character portrayals. Understand the choices they make to bring their characters to life. You have to watch films and read plays that were released twenty, thirty, even fifty years ago, not just those that came out in the last year. This process will train your eyes and ears, and help you dissect every movie, play, and television show you watch. Your days of watching for pure enjoyment have ended. Every time you watch something or read a script, you are building your knowledge and expanding your frame of reference. You will learn, as part of the craft of acting, to pick out the role you would be cast in, even if it's the role of a waitress or cab driver with one line. Part of your training is learning to develop your niche and answer the question, "How do you see yourself and what roles do you see yourself playing?"

DAWN

As an actress, one of the questions always presented to me was, "How do you see yourself?" I was never able to answer and when I did, it was always a cop-out. "I see myself as the quirky, zany best friend." And yes, zany and quirky are a part of me; but they were not my essence, and not the statement I wanted to make. Quirky and zany were my overcompensation, my mask. By being animated, I never had to show my vulnerability or my discomfort. I took no real risks and I reaped no real rewards. The more ditsy and zany I acted, the more I strayed from my true self, the self I so desperately wanted to show

As a child, I identified with tragic roles. I wanted to play these roles to express what I couldn't in real life. But I was too scared to expose myself, so instead I would do a one hundred and eighty degree turn. I would portray myself as Lucille Ball meets Gidget. The real me was lost. I didn't know how to let myself be raw, vulnerable, or ugly. Growing up my mother was constantly telling me, "Be strong. Beautiful women are strong." In my house, strong was interpreted as emotionless. If you would let an emotion surface, you would be perceived as weak and weak women are not attractive. My mother's voice always resonated in me louder than my own. I disagreed with everything she said; yet, I was frozen by the echoing of her words. I did not have the emotional freedom to allow my own voice to surface. I was stifled and it stifled my emotional range as an actress.

One of the amazing things about acting is it allows you the freedom to voice yourself through the author's words. You can say anything without repercussion. A role allows you to express yourself through someone else's words. Text gives you *role distance*, a separation between you and the role you portray, allowing you to live as someone else and then walk away. A skilled actor knows how to separate the role from his life. I had not developed this skill, of really living in the moment. According to Sanford Meisner, creator of the Meisner Technique, "…acting is reacting, living moment to moment…" When I spoke with photographer Robert Zuckerman, he repeatedly said, "Actors make a strong statement when, without judgment or criticism, they can just be themselves. Actors don't need to mug for the camera or pretend they have a certain intensity. When they look at you, they reveal a part of who they are." Not all actors can do this. It is a gift to remain natural in unnatural circumstances. Flaws, openness, and candor are an actor's beauty. As an actor, you need to be comfortable with these "special" aspects of yourself and learn how to meta-morphasize and transform them in the roles and characters you portray. A good actor reveals. He allows you to see his soul through the character's mask. According to Robert, the most successful headshots are created when an actor doesn't ask the photographer to change who they are. "…if a character type comes in and tells me she wants to look like an ingenue, I tell her I'm probably not the right photographer for her; my photos are reflections. When casting directors see my work, they know that the actor in the picture is going to be the actor who walks in the door. The picture is an honest statement of the person, not an artificially enhanced, airbrushed version."

During our conversation, Robert commented on what a good listener I was. He said the way I listened was refreshing and non judgmental. I was taken aback. I was merely listening. At that moment, I realized what it was I was never able to do as an actress—just listen and be. At my audition for *Death of a Salesman*, Arthur Miller asked me repeatedly to stop moving, speaking, and gesturing .He eventually made me stand on stage silent and motionless. It seemed like an eternity. He instructed me to make eye contact with each and every person in the audience. To really look at them and let them really look at me. When I got to him, he looked at me so intensely I began to cry. As I was standing up there in tears, embarrassed, afraid, and emotionally naked, he told me *that moment*, when I was absolutely still, is what I needed to embrace. "That is acting!" I never understood Mr. Miller's words until Robert looked at me and said, "He enjoyed my stillness."

What I now understand is that to answer the question, "How do you see yourself?" I didn't need to look so hard. I just had to take a deep breath and let my true colors emerge.

Creating your image through hair, make-up and clothes.
A 12-step plan to creating a haircut that helps define your image according to
Yutaka of Yutaka Hair Salon in West Hollywood

> **Yutaka**
> **371 N. La Cienega**
> **West Hollywood**
> *(310) 652-0127*

- I believe it's important to learn about the personality of the person before you talk about a cut. I like to know the person's goals, likes and lifestyle.

- After I talk to a person for a little bit, I look at their hair to understand their texture to minimize problems later.

- Wet hair to see the hair's natural flow.

- Discuss the type of work the client is going for—commercial, high fashion, or theatrical work.

- Look at the person's book and/or headshots to see what looks have worked for them in the past.

- I suggest the styles that I think would look good on the person.

- I discuss the type of clothing and make-up that they wear daily.

- I discuss the styling methods they use at home

- I ask about their preferences for managing their looks, i.e. do they use conditioner, toner, blow dry their hair, etc.

- Discuss whether they want to change the color of their hair or just add highlights.

- I tell them to think about it for a couple of days and not make a rash decision.

- Get to work on creating the incredible style, cut and color that will get them working in the business.

OTHER HAIRDRESSERS WE LIKE

Fredrick Fekai
440 N. Rodeo Drive
(310) 777-8700
Beverly Hills
pricey but excellent
See: Yoshee

Jonathan Salon
901 Westbourne
West Hollywood
(310) 855-0225
Pricey but excellent
See: Jonathan

L Salon
7151 Beverly Blvd.
LA, CA
(323) 930-0700
Specializes in color & cutting
See: Marty (he will do house calls
for special clients)

Marks and Michael's
8277 Melrose Ave
(323) 852-1602 / (323) 651-0811
Excellent for hair color & Afro-
American styling; reasonable prices
see :Raymond or Michael

Next Salon
2400 Main Street
Santa Monica, CA
(310) 392-6645
Excellent cuts and color
See: Noori

Off The Top
1418 Main Street
Venice CA
(310) 452-8985
See: Andrea

Prive Salon
7373 Beverly Blvd.
West Hollywood
(323) 931-5559
Laurent D—celebrity stylist; takes a
couple of weeks to book an appointment, but well worth the wait

Umberto Salon
416 Canon Drive
Beverly Hills, CA
(310) 274 –6395
See: Sammy

Vandii
648 N. Martel
West Hollywood, CA
(323) 651-3498
See: Donny—specializes in cutting ,
male & female; reasonable prices

Wilder Brothers
7975 Melrose Blvd
West Hollywood, CA
(323) 653-4407
See: Tom excellent for custom wigs

Put Your Best Face Forward! The best make-up starts with good skin and properly shaped brows. Below are the best place for facials, make-up applications, and brow shaping.

FACIALS

Burke Williams—Complete Spa
8000 W.Sunset Blvd.
LA, CA
(323) 822-9007

Sonia Dekar Skin Clinic
8309 Beverly Blvd.
West Hollywood
(323) 655-3061
Great facials; relaxing atmosphere, makes her own products

Enessa
8012 ½ Melrose
West Hollywood, CA
(323) 655-5950
See: Michelle (she's the best in town)
Great attitude, all natural products, reasonably priced; aromatherapy.

Vera's Retreat
2980 Beverly Glen Circle
(310) 470-6362

EYEBROW WAXING

Anastasia
438 N. Bedford Drive
(310) 273-3155

Valerie of Beverly Hills
460 N. Canon Drive
(310) 274-7348

MAKE-UP

Fred Segal
8100 Melrose Ave.
West Hollywood
(323) 651-0239
The counter girls are excellent with latest brands.

MAC PRO
133 North Robertson Blvd.
West Hollywood, CA
(310) 271-9137
Union actors receive a 30% discount with $35 membership card.

Senna Cosmetics
N. Camden
(310) 274-1028
Ask for Eugenia Westin

Valerie of Beverly Hills
460 N. Canon Drive
Beverly Hills, CA
(310) 274-7348
Try to book a make-up application with Valerie herself. It's hard to get an appointment; so if you can't wait, ask for a recommendation for one of her other artists. Her make-up is also the best.

PHOTOGRAPHERS THAT CAN HELP ENVISION YOUR IMAGE

Sara Corwin Photography
West Hollywood
(323) 655-5705
price includes hair & makeup

Delucia Photography
(310) 394-1409

Bob Libens Photography
Hollywood
(323) 876-2977
Very Reasonable. Satisfaction guaranteed.

Mindas Photography
14106 Ventura Blvd., Sherman Oaks
(818) 905-5866

Deano Mueller Photography
Hollywood
(323) 465-6818

Gina Nemo Photography
(310) 454-4122
Will shoot on location

Patina Rodgers Photography
West LA
(310) 393-7252
Very personable

Doug Schneeman Photography
Van Nuys
(818) 786-0213
Reasonable rates

Ute Ville
West Hollywood
(323) 658-6574

Shandon Young Claus Studio
Downtown LA
(818) 766-8389

Photographers 'addresses have been omitted to protect their privacy. Must call for appointment.

DUPLICATING SERVICES WITH QUALITY

Anderson Graphics, Inc.
6037 Woodman Ave., Van Nuys
(818) 909-9100

Image Starters
8159 Santa Monica Blvd.
(818) 506-7010

Final Print
1952 North Van Ness, Hollywood
(323) 466-0566
(818) 285-6967
(310) 979-7884

Graphic Reproductions
1421 N. Labrea, W. HWD
(323) 874-4335

Prints Charmin, Inc.
11657 Sawtelle Blvd., LA
(310) 312-0904

Producers & Quantity (P&Q)
6660 Santa Monica Blvd.
(323) 462-1334

Ray—The Actors Lab
1330 N. Highland Ave, HWD
(323) 463-0555
(818) 760-3656
Retouching

Sir Speedy
6660 W. Sunset Blvd., LA
(323) 469-0327
Model cards—Zed cards

RESUME, PRINTING, VIDEOTAPE EDITING AND DUPLICATION

Barbara's Place
7925 Santa Monica Blvd., W. HWD
(323) 654-5012
Great for resumes

Charlie Chan Printing
8267 Santa Monica Blvd., W. HWD
(323) 650-7699
Ask for Hai or Mai
Resumes, business cards, laser prints at
Reasonable prices.

Allen Fawcett's Sound Stage
4962 Alcove Ave., N. HWD
North Hollywood
(818)763-8252
Free consultation for demo tape and
great editing.

Gosh Productions.Com
2227 West Olive, Burbank
(818) 729-0000

Great place to edit demo reels
Ask for Jeremy

Jan's Video
1800 Argyle, W. HWD
(323) 462-5511
Very skillful in editing demo reels

Kinkos—Open 24 hours
Hollywood (323) 845-4501—
Studio City (818) 980-2679-
Van Nuys (818) 780-2123
Printing, resumes, business cards,
laser, but they are expensive.

Potty Mouth Productions.Com
(323) 428-7333—cell
(818) 846-1779—studio
David McClellan
Good editor

Twenty Questions to Ask Yourself To Determine Your Castability

❑ Are you a comedian or a dramatic person?

❑ Are you more comfortable in the genre of comedy or drama?

❑ In your own life, do you deal with emotions and stressful situations through drama or comedy?

❑ In school, were you the straight man or the clown?

❑ Are you an ingenue, a character type or the girl next door?

❑ Are you a leading man or the zany best friend type?

❑ What is your favorite movie and the character whom you most relate to?

❑ Are you considered all American or more ethnic?

❑ What emotions are you most comfortable at expressing?

❑ What emotions are you least comfortable expressing?

❑ What is it you feel you need to convey as an actor?

❑ How do other people type you?

❑ What are the qualities you most like about yourself?

❑ Are you realistic about the parts that you can play?

❑ What qualities make you unique, i.e. when you laugh you squeal a little bit?

❑ Do you feel you have a wide range as an actor?

❑ Where do you get your strengths from? Your weaknesses?

❑ What can you bring to the part you're auditioning for that is unique?

❑ If you don't look like how you feel, how are you going to modify and come to terms with this inconsistency?

❑ Can you do period pieces? Accents?

Casting Worksheet

Write a brief paragraph or two about the roles you see yourself playing in movies, plays, & TV. Why?

Example: I see myself playing Rose in Titanic because I have an old world sensibility and a yearning for passion in my life.

 **Ten Things I did This Month To Begin Creating My Image :**

1. _____

2. _____

3. _____

4. _____

5. _____

6. _____

7. _____

8. _____

9. _____

10. _____

10 Things I Did This Month That I'm Proud Of:

1. _____

2. _____

3. _____

4. _____

5. _____

6. _____

7. _____

8. _____

9. _____

10. _____

CHAPTER 6

Step Six, Month Six

Six Month Reflections

> "Go to the edge," he said. "No." she said. "I will fall."
> "Go to the edge," he said. "No." she said. "I will fall."
> "She walked to the edge."
> "He pushed her."
> "And she flew."
>
> —Anonymous

If you are still reading, you have made the commitment to stay in LA and pursue your professional acting career. You have set up your new home, you are studying, you have explored the town, you have a great headshot, and you have made some friends and contacts. The previous steps have helped lay the foundation for you to start pounding the pavement in pursuit of agent representation and you're beginning to work as a professional actor. The next six months will probably be very difficult. You have chosen a career where rejection is a part of your daily life. However, there are ways to combat this.

The security of a schedule, a support system, and a home to go to will give you the necessary piece of mind essential for the second phase of your first year.

Chapter six is designed to help you during this transition phase—getting out there, auditioning and working as a professional actor. We have created this chapter in order to give you some breathing time to take a personal inventory and reflect on all the changes that have occurred over the last six months. The changes have been immense, both personally and professionally. Get prepared, like it or not, rejection is about to become a big part of your daily life. Now is a crucial time to learn the skills necessary for dealing with rejection and the art of transforming it. No experience is a negative one, if you understand how to process it. This knowledge will help keep you emotionally and spiritually grounded, inspired and on track, provided that an acting career and your life go hand in hand. Always remember that rejection is merely someone's opinion of your castability of a particular role. It is not a statement of your being. Even actors of celebrity status deal with rejection. It is imperative to know how to transform others' opinions of you and your work. This will be a key in determining your success in this often ruthless and highly competitive business.

The worksheets provided at the end of this chapter are essential. They will be your best friends during these hard times. The exercises are not mysterious and they do not require you to delve into the psychology of your past lives. We will not ask you to read any Freud or Shirley McClaine unless you want to. However, this chapter is work. It is a part of the step plan, part of your personal tool kit in building your dreams.

The exercises are a meat and potatoes approach to dealing with the stresses and wavering emotions. These problems will occur more than you would like. Highs and lows are to be expected for an actor. Learning to take care of your person and your emotional self is an essential task. Without this tool kit, you will not be able to survive the battles that will be required of you in order to win the war. This career choice is one of extreme joy, disappointment, frustration, unemployment versus too much employment, as well as the simple stresses of life. These worksheets, journal pages, and inventory lists will save your life, keeping you centered and true to plan. Use them religiously. They will be your bible to sanity, balance and success.

In earlier chapters, we encouraged you to recognize and acknowledge your accomplishments. Now we want to encourage you to create a serious inventory of all the positive actions you have taken since you have arrived in LA. This inventory is extremely important. It will help you focus as well as reflect back on all that you have accomplished over the last six months. You might think that you are aware of all your accomplishments, but you will be amazed at all you have done when you read back your list. The simple act of putting your goals on paper is a visible declaration of your focus and determination. Your inventory should include everything from finding a home to simply getting together with a partner from one of your acting classes to mastering the *Thomas Guide*. These isolated events that at first appeared unconnected are now linked and become deposits in what can be called your emotional savings account. Every time you make a deposit, it reinforces your present successes— where you are now and where you want to be in the future. From now on, view every deposit, big or small, as fuel that increases your self-esteem and your emotional determination to move forward.

Dawn

As a therapist, I have worked with a variety of clients on personal awareness and self esteem. A common thread with all the different clients is that people have a hard time articulating their feelings. They usually can talk about a situation or a problem that one of their friend's have, but when it comes to stating a simple truth about how they are feeling, even the most gregarious person retreats. A simple technique to combat this is the **"I Feel" exercise**. It works wonderfully before and after auditions.

The "I feel" statement is one of the easiest ways to take your emotional temperature. It is as simple as stating a one-word adjective—angry, lonely, mad, frustrated, happy, funny, etc. It is important before you walk into the audition room to know what your emotional temperature is, so you know how to work with it accordingly. Both going in and leaving an audition, stay emotionally connected to your feelings. Learn how to identify and own whatever emotion is present—transform it, then release it. This exercise is simple yet effective. It is one of several exercises you can learn. If you are not adept at dealing with emotions on your own, find or form a support group with your peers. This is a wonderful way to establish a sense of stability in this unstable world of Hollywood and acting.

Designing your group

Make a definite time and place to meet each week—"consistency is important." You are creating a structure and a safe place. Agree on a leader and a list of group members. This group is a place where you should feel supported to talk about your week and your progress.

The structure of any good group has three phases: Warm-up, Enactment and Closure. *Warm-up* is where the group members check in and assess how they are doing. It's the icebreaker. *Enactment* is the structured activity or meat and potatoes of the group. *Closure* is the validation that enables each and every member to leave with a renewed feeling of confidence. It gives everyone the hope to fight through to the next week.

There are many types of groups, each with different goals. Decide if your group deals solely with emotional issues or whether it is a more career oriented, networking group where actors can share their audition experiences and stories. The networking group is more task oriented. We will provide exercises for leading both types of groups as well as work sheets, journal pages, questions, and the best spas and yoga places in town which is my favorite way to combat stress. Feel free to create your own exercises as well as the exercises we provide.

When I was a new actress in LA, I found that access to a support group was amazing in keeping me excited and positive. It was both informative, insightful, social, and a place that just understood me like no other. Not to be corny, but it's true. This group gave me a sense of belonging and something to look forward to when my week was not going as I had hoped. Groups are grounding and give direction regardless of the type. Find one or create your own!

Warm Up Exercise

The warm up phase is essential in every group. If you begin every session with this, you will create an atmosphere of continuity and safety. Whoever leads the group should sit in the circle with all the other members. This is called the warm up circle. It is the time to create and establish a supportive creative rapport.

Exercise: Warm up Exercise

Goals—Create a supportive atmosphere and loosen up the group for the work to come.

Steps:

1. Invite all the participants to sit in a circle on the floor.

2. Have every group member take a moment to settle in and make eye contact with everyone else in the circle

3. Ask everyone to sit up straight, close his or her eyes and breathe in and out in a relaxed manner.

4. Begin to lead the group in a couple of easy stretches, first from the sitting position with head rolls, ankle stretches and facial stretches, etc. Then do some standing exercises, swinging arms in circles, stretching the back, and lifting the knees. Don't make it into a yoga class, these aren't for physical fitness, just relaxing the mind.

5. Softly give the group the instructions for the next activity, whether it be an action oriented exercise or a just a discussion, presentation, or lecture.

Enactment Exercises

Exercise: The Negative Messages

Goals—To understand the impact that negative messages have on us and to learn to release them.

Steps:

1. Find a few pieces of paper

2. Ask a partner to trace around you and draw your outline on the paper

3. List all the negative messages you have either heard of or felt at auditions at the top of your picture. For example, too short, too tall, not funny enough.

4. Share these with the group.

Exercise: Letting Go of Judgment

Goals—A guided imagery for letting go of judgment

Lie on you back with your palms facing upwards or sit in a comfortable position. Let your breath flow in and out, filling you with a sense of ease and softness and light. Allow any tension you may be storing to leave your body—breath out and relax. Breathe in and out easily and completely without a pause between inhalation and exhalation. Mentally move through your body locating any areas of tension and directing those muscles to let go. Allow your mind to drift to a peaceful place. Let any distracting thoughts simply disappear onto the horizon and allow yourself to go deeper and deeper. Imagine yourself doing something you feel awkward doing or that you feel you do badly. See yourself as you struggle through this activity. Watch yourself feel the embarrassment that you experience at these times. Tune into your hearing until you can hear the voices of judgment that are running through your mind. Slow down your awareness so that you can hear the exact words that the voices are saying. They may be the same words over and over again or they may be several voices. Listen for one message that is stronger than all the rest. What is it saying? Who is saying it? Place those words in a large container and remove them from the place where they are in your mind.

What would you like to do with those words? Do it now, in any way that feels comfortable. Take inner action towards those words. Good.

Now whatever forms the words are in, wrap them up and let them rise up, up and away from your consciousness. It was only something someone said not a statement of your being. Let them go and forgive yourself for having taken them into your heart. They need no longer have power over you. Understand that the person who said them is not you and need not control you in anyway. Let them go!! Forgive all. Say to yourself, "I am my own best friend. I will treat myself with kindness. I will protect my heart." Slowly, whenever you feel ready, bring your consciousness back into the room. And when you are ready open your eyes.

Record in your journal the feelings that arose during this exercise. You may keep it to yourself or share it with the group.

Exercise: I Am the Goal

Goal—Seeing yourself in a goal

Steps:

1. Pass out paper, markers, pens and crayons, and have the group write or draw three goals that they have for themselves over the next five years.

2. Everyone picks a partner and shares your paper with them.

3. Come back to the circle and have your partner share your goals if you feel that you are comfortable enough sharing with the group.

4. Discuss any emotions or feeling that arose during the sharing phase.

Exercise: Relaxation

Goal—To achieve productive relaxation, either alone or in a group.

Steps:

1. Lie on your back with your palms at your side.

2. Breathe in and out.

3. Relax your body while maintaining your breathing. Feel your breath move through your forehead, eyes, cheeks, mouth, tongue, jaw, chest, finger tips, waist, hips, legs, feet, and lastly toes.

4. As you breathe, release any negative emotions that occurred throughout the day.

Exercise: Journal Writing Exercise

Goal—To release feelings in a safe way and gain insight into your own psyche.

Steps:

1. Pick up your journal and a pen.

2. Begin to write; allow whatever you are feeling to surface.

3. Write whatever comes to mind in an uncensored way. Do not edit anything that comes up.

Exercise: Affirmations

Goal—Replace old negative messages with new positive ones.

Steps:

1. Center yourself and listen to positive affirmation tapes.
2. Center yourself and read daily affirmations from a book.
3. Write down any affirmations you need for the rest of the day.
4. Place affirmations in your apartment, car, and office.

Exercise: Mirroring

Goal—To see yourself through someone else.

Steps:

1. Find a partner
2. Center yourself and just look at your partner.
3. Observe your partner's eyes, forehead, and body placement.
4. One person be the mirror the other be the facilitator of the action. The facilitator makes slow large had and facial gestures. The person who is the mirror follows along doing exactly what the facilitator is doing.
5. Switch partners.
6. Discuss the feelings that arouse during this activity.

Exercise: The Inner and Outer Mask

Goal—To bring confidential information into the circle and share it with the group.

Steps:

1. Hand out large pieces of paper and colored markers
2. Draw two pictures. The first is the person you present to the outside world. The second is the person beneath the mask.
3. On the side of the pictures write these words; I feel…I look…I am…I need…I never…I am afraid of…and complete the phrase.
4. Share your picture with the book

Exercise: Closure Exercise

Goal—To close the group and share and validate what was experienced.

Steps:

1. Reform the circle from the warm-up phase.
2. Go around the circle and ask everyone to share what they experienced in the group. In sharing do not criticize others. Say what came up for you.
3. Thank everyone for their work and tell them when the next group will meet again.

SHAPE YOUR BODY & WATCH OTHER PEOPLE SHAPE THEIRS

Bally's (many locations...actors hang out Studio City)
1135 Ventura Blvd.
1 800 846-0256
Studio City, CA

Beverly Hills Health and Fitness
(a fun laid back kind of atmosphere, no posers)
8301 Beverly Blvd.
West Hollywood
(323) 658-6999
Always running special membership deals. Open 24 hours.

Bodies in Motion
7021 Hollywood Blvd., Hollywood
(323) 462-0299
Great boxing training

Crunch
8000 Sunset Blvd.
West Hollywood, CA
(323) 654-4550
Great classes. Great networking.

Family Fitness
9911 W. Pico
LA CA (near Century City)
(310) 553-7600

Gold's Gym
(where you can see all the ultimate in muscles; Arnold started there)
360 Hampton Drive
Venice, CA 90291
(310) 392-6004
1016 N. Cole
Hollywood
(323) 462-7012

The Powerhouse Gym
11400 West Olympic
West LA, CA
(310) 854-7700
Great state of the art equipment

Sports Club LA
1835 S. Sepulveda
LA, CA
(310) 473-1447
Trendy, lots of attitude, lots of make-up

The Greatest Places To Take A Break From The Rat-Race, Relax And Pamper Yourself

Aida Thebian European Spa
449 N. Cannon Drive
Beverly Hills
(310) 278-7565
A complete full service spa.
Pricey but well worth it.

Beverly Hills Hot Springs
308 North Oxford Ave.
Hollywood, CA
(323) 734-7000
Massages, facials and baths…sepa-
rating the men from the ladies, this
place will take all your cares away.
You'll definitely feel refreshed and
relaxed.

Burke Williams
8000 W. Sunset Blvd
(323) 822-9007
A complete and luxurious full service spa. Bowls of fruit and bottled
water served free. Pricey but you can
get half-hour facial for $55.

Enessa
8012 ½ Melrose Ave.
Run by the nurturing Michelle
Orenstein. Her boutique provides the

best facials, massages, and hair
removal services in a relaxing and
therapeutic atmosphere. Her products are amazing too. She makes
them herself and they're all aromatherapy based. The whole experience is wonderful. A must experience.
West Hollywood
(323) 655-5950

Ole Henriksen Face/Body
8622 Sunset Blvd.
LA, CA
Complimentary Eucalyptus Steam
Room with any service.
Hydrotherapy Room. Great facials
but pricey.
(310) 854-7700

Yoga Works
2215 Main Street
Santa Monica CA
(310) 393-5150
A hot spot for all levels of yoga
goers. A favorite among
Hollywood's A list.

The Twenty Questions To Ask Yourself About Your Progress Over The Last Six Months

- ❏ What were your personal goals for the last six months?
- ❏ What were your professional goals for the last six months?
- ❏ What were your financial goals for the last six months?
- ❏ What accomplishments are you most proud of in the last six months?
- ❏ Did anything happen in the last six months that you regret?
- ❏ Do you feel you are on the right career path?
- ❏ Are you still excited about pursuing your acting career in LA?
- ❏ Do you like LA?
- ❏ Are you happy with your living arrangement?
- ❏ Have you secured a steady job?
- ❏ Have you made any friends?
- ❏ Are you happy with your acting class?
- ❏ Do you have a definite idea of your type and how to market yourself?
- ❏ Have you taken some leisure time to explore LA?
- ❏ Do you feel your life in LA is well balanced?
- ❏ What have you been doing for fun?
- ❏ Are you reading the trades every week?
- ❏ Do you have a monologue you are ready to perform?
- ❏ Do you have a scene you are ready to perform?
- ❏ Can you write a five-minute biographical piece about your relocation and your experiences thus far?

CHAPTER 7

Month Seven, Step Seven

Mailings That Get Results

> "Talk about the right picture at the right time...I looked at many photos to match 'young Ryan' in <u>Saving Private Ryan</u>. I came across Harrison Young's portrait and saw those eyes. But could he act? I had him do a reading and he broke my heart. I was very lucky to find him."
> —Steven Spielberg (as told to Harrison Young)

> I did my first Broadway show in 1974. I have been doing mailings for 23 years waiting for this wonderful part. It goes to show that one must never give up.
> —Harrison Young, *Saving Private Ryan*

They say a picture is worth a thousand words. This is especially true when you are doing mailings to agents, managers, producers and casting directors. It is the first thing they see. It is your calling card, so make sure it looks professional. This is not the place to skimp on expenses or expose your best friend's work who is taking his first photography class. Headshot photos are a necessary investment, so take the adequate amount of time to save up your money and review different photographers' books. At the end of Chapter Five, we have provided you with a list of photographers as well as helpful tips for your photo shoot.

As we mentioned in Chapter Five, your picture needs to make a personal statement about you and what you represent. Are you a character type, an ingenue, the next Jennifer Aniston, Cameron Diaz, Matthew Perry, Leonardo DeCaprio or the girl next door? This does not mean you do not have range as an actor, it just means know who you are as a casting type and target the appropriate roles that you are right for. You are your own company, and your picture and resume are your company's brochure. So target the proper buyer by sending the proper brochure.

An actor can have more than one head shot. Most actors have a commercial shot (a picture used for commercial representation and commercial auditions) and a theatrical shot (a more dramatic shot for theater and film roles).

One of the most important ingredients in any successful headshot is the person's essence—that "special something" that makes them unique. It's not about having the most beautiful flawless picture. It is about the personality that illuminates, the spirit that shines through. The picture should step out and say, "Hello! There is something I need to say."

It's important to be very detailed in your mailings. Be sure you have the proper spelling of the person you are mailing your photo and résumé. Stick to the specific requirements the person requested in their listing. Mention whether you received the material first hand or through a source book like the *Ross Report, The Agencies,* or *The Back Stage Handbook For The Performing Artists,* (all of which provide the information on who's who and what's what in the agent, manager, casting world). And most importantly use the right amount of postage; otherwise…well you know.

The *Ross Report* and *The Agencies* are the most commonly used reference sources in the business for mailings since they are constantly being updated. They list the names of all the agencies with the names of who does what within each of the companies. *The Ross Report,* which lists all prime time series being cast, is a must. It also tells you what agents and casting people are open to receiving pictures and resumes and if they require tape (a half—inch video of your work. At this point in your career you may not have one. If you don't, it's O.K. You will in good time.) Later in Chapter 11, we will discuss making your tape, how, where and the possible benefits.

Above all, the first thing in your package that gets glanced at is your picture, so make sure it looks like *you*—not some idealized, airbrushed image that you might have in your head or wish for with some plastic surgery. To check this, sometimes it can be helpful to ask someone you do not know that well. Sometimes strangers can be more objective than people we are close to.

COVER LETTERS

If you include a note with your picture and resume, make it short, sweet and to the point. Find a way to make it catchy, yet still professional—whether it be your paper choice, style of writing, humor, page layout, etc. Just stick to the point and save your novel writing for the literary agents' submissions.

This package is your calling card! Entice your audience; leave them wanting to know more. Just like in a scene, know the motivation for your mailing. Why are you doing the mailing? Who are you mailing to and what do you want to accomplish? Make sure to answer the twenty questions at the end of the chapter before you sit down to prepare your package.

TIPS

*Two of the best places for an actor in LA, or anywhere else, happens to be a thespian specialty shop called **Samuel French** and **Larry Edmund's**. Inside these special bookstores, you can find scripts from almost any film. There are more selections of full-length plays and one acts then anyplace else. Not only will you be able to find that script you've been looking for at both these place; but you can also get helpful advice from the employees, purchase resource books and directories like **The Agencies**, the **Ross Report**, and **The Working Actors Guide** as well as many other books that list agents and casting offices. These guides are invaluable because they are constantly updating agent and casting office information. Samuel French even has pre-printed mailing labels for managers, agents, and casting offices, which will save your hand from a lot of writing. Although it will save you precious time, it may also cost a bit. Basically, these two stores carry every iota of information and materials you may need for a large mailing of headshots and resumes and much, much more.*

The Twenty Questions You Need To Ask Yourself For Mailings That Get Results

❑ What do I want to accomplish from this mailing, i.e. getting an audition for an existing part in an independent film, commercial, music video, or a general meeting with an agent, manager, or casting director?

❑ Am I following up with someone I met in a social setting?

❑ Is this a connection a friend or family member gave me?

❑ Am I responding mostly to castings listed in a trade paper?

❑ Have I been mailing to agents and managers?

❑ Have I mailed to this company or person before?

❑ If I've mailed to this person before, do I have something new to inform them of?

❑ Am I going to hand write the note or type it?

❑ Do I know anything personal or special about this individual or company to include in the note?

❑ Is the role I'm submitting for comedy or drama and does the note reflect the persona of the character?

❑ Do I feel that the headshot I'm sending captures the essence of the role I want to audition for?

❑ Are you using the proper postage?

❑ Did you double check the proper spelling of person's name and addresses your are targeting?

❑ Are you making a checklist of everyone you're mailing to so you can follow-up?

❑ If you are sending for a stylized show that's already on the air, does your package mimic that style?

❑ If you were to receive your own package, what would you think?

❑ What do your friends think of your mailing? What about a stranger?

❑ Are you dedicating two hours a week to mailings?

❑ Are you following up on your mailings with postcards?

❑ How can I improve my response rate?

BONUS TIP: Don't get sick from licking the envelopes. Use a sponge.

CHAPTER 8

Month Eight, Step Eight

Agent Interviews

Since your agent gets 10% of your earnings
your agent does 10% of the work
The actor must do the other 90%

—Commercial Actor

I give my actors 90% of what I earn for them!

—Commercial Agent

Your mailing paid off. Congratulations! You have the interview—If this is your first meeting with an agent or manager, outstanding! If you have traveled this road before, your dedication and focus also need to be acknowledged. We want you to recognize what you have achieved thus far and appreciate the work that has gone into reaching this goal. Celebrate each and every victory, big or small, by giving your accomplishments the weight they deserve.

From our experience, the simple act of getting in the door accounts for more than half the battle in getting representation. What you do once you get in the room depends on how prepared you are creatively and personally.

This chapter is designed to guide you through the interview process. You need to learn what to expect and what is expected of you. We cannot give you every possible scenario, but we can get you to the point where you should be able to handle whatever is thrown your way.

When you go into the interview, remember: This is a team effort and you are responsible for creating and designing your career as much as your agent. Your work is done in conjunction with the agent, not in spite of them. You need to constantly promote yourself. You need to find new, imaginative ways to get your name and talent in front of the people who can hire you. Do not look at the agent's daily submission of your photograph and resume as the be-all in your quest for the job. They submit, they follow-up, and they push and use their relationships to get work for you as well as their other clients.

You are, or will become, one of possibly hundreds of actors the agency represents on a daily basis. Some of these actors earn the lion's share of attention because they bring in the most money—they sustain the company. Their abilities also attract casting people, directors, and producers who are looking to hire additional actors, such as yourself, from the agency's client list.

This does not mean you should stand on the sideline and bow your head in reverence to the working or "established" actor. On the contrary, now is the time to develop another strategy but with someone, your agent. These are the people you have agreed to take on as your representative. They are in the position to further your career and bring you to the next level, but they can—not do this alone.

Find out in your interview and succeeding conversations what they need from you. Discover, from their point of view, what you can do to make their job easier.

You cannot succeed by yourself—again, this is a team effort. Do not think for a moment that having an agent is going to change everything for you. The only thing that has changed is that you are in a position to gain the support of a company—a name that gives you credibility and visibility.

Agents do not create miracles out of thin air. They need the materials to produce. You are the material, the product that they market day in and day out. Give them the best quality possible. Make sure their needs and wants are taken care of—from having enough great headshots, to staying in regular communication. Take responsibility for your career.

An agency, regardless of its size, receives hundreds of submissions a week from actors in search of representation. There is no guarantee your headshot and demo tape, (if you have one to submit), will be reviewed, but put your best foot forward, and refer back to chapter seven before you do your mailing.

An agent's job is to discover new talent and sign recognizable names that will bring notoriety and money into the agency. However, their responsibility, first and foremost is to their clients. Those individuals they have signed or are "hip-pocketed" (actors an agency or agent chooses to work with on the side without signing them). This is done to determine, via two or three auditions, whether the actor has what it takes to work without the agent having to invest much of their time or energy on their immediate career.

Actors, by their very nature, need and want to feel as though they are the only clients that matter. They want to be taken care of, they want their calls returned, and they want to go out and audition.

A good agent, more often than not, will be able to supply that type of relationship to everyone at all times—regardless of how overwhelming the task may be. Although there comes a time when it's impossible for them to field every call and question. If they were to answer every question, they would not be getting you auditions.

As an aspiring actor, you need to know that agents are constantly submitting your headshots for projects, following up on submissions, negotiating deals, and meeting with the other agents in the company while simultaneously counseling, promoting, instructing, and guiding their actors. This is all in a day's work, not to mention the work done outside the office—going to screenings of new films, plays and dinner meetings. In addition to reading one or two scripts a night, he is talking with producers and directors about upcoming projects. This is a twenty-four hour a day, seven days a week job. So be to the point and be prepared with a pen and paper when you call; there is nothing worse than a disorganized actor.

THE INTERVIEW

The first and most important thing is your attitude. That is the first thing that is noticed in any interview, in any situation. Depending on your attitude, it could be over before it begins.

Questions the agent might ask at your initial meeting: "…So, what have you done lately?" "Tell me about yourself…Why are we meeting?" These direct and seemingly innocuous questions can strike fear in the heart of any newcomer if they are not prepared. This is your time to shine so make the most of it.

Think of this meeting as if it were a first date. You want to look a certain way that not only makes you feel comfortable with yourself but also makes you attractive to the other person—in this case, the agent. You would not go out with someone for the evening and present yourself as a person who is totally void of humor, thoughts or feelings—would you? The same is true for any meetings you are going out on. In both instances, they want to see you. They want you to be the person they will fall in love with. They want to learn who you are—so reveal. Tell them where you come from, what you have been doing. You want to put your best foot forward and show that you are more than just another actor in Los Angeles. Be yourself; let them see what you are really like. Talk about things you enjoy— what sports for instance—and be willing to express your knowledge or feelings about the subject, say the NFL or NBA. This does not mean putting on a song and dance routine or sharing your innermost secrets, but it does mean letting the colors of your personality out and revealing who you are. You do not have to *try* to be interesting. The agent will be attracted to you and consequently attracted to your talent and potential.

The work you did earlier with regard to casting, setting yourself up in a class, etc. all comes into play at this moment. Remember, people are interesting, actors can be boring. The agent wants to see that you are a real person, not just an actor or an "actortron" pretending to be a human being. Like the date, talk with the person, communicate and share ideas. It's the only way you will discover if this is the person you want to set up shop with. In the process, show you have a handle, a certain understanding of what the business is about, and how you possibly see yourself fitting in. Discuss the roles you see yourself playing. Ask them how they see you. It may be too much to learn in the first meeting, but learn as much as you can.

Above all, your attitude once again will determine how you are perceived. Do not go into the meeting feeling like a second-class citizen. Never allow that voice in your head, which yaps on about how you do not have as much to offer as someone else, take control of the meeting. And never apologize for what you have or have not yet accomplished.

No one is doing you a favor when they call you in. So while you should be happy for the opportunity, do not act as though you are taking up their "valuable time"—regardless of how you obtained the meeting. This is your time. Let yourself be the "star." Take charge, but do not be controlling. Be interested in what they have to say, and how they perceive you. They should know more by the sheer fact they have been in the business longer.

In the end, if they do not have all the answers, that's okay. If you don't have all the answers—fine. Nobody expects you to. You are learning. This is a process. If you make a mistake, the floor will not open up and suck you into some sort of actor purgatory. You are not going to hit a home run every time. So relax and let yourself be you. You will make some mistakes, but don't worry. In the next chapter, we will provide some after interview techniques.

Give it your best shot. As you leave the interview, accept what happened; take notes on your journal pages—what you felt positive about, what you can possibly improve on for the next time. There will be a next time, and then you let it go. Remember, you're in LA—never more than twenty minutes from the beach.

When all is said and done, a meeting is only an exchange of ideas and feelings between people who are interested in each other. It is a forum that allows people to learn more about who the other person is, and discuss how together, each can reach the same goal.

If by the end of the meeting you mutually decide to work together, make sure you understand the contracts and commissions. Take them home, study them, ask a friend—maybe even a lawyer if you know one. If you or the agent wants to think about it for a couple of days, that's fine too. There is no race to the finish line, so take the time you need and find out all the information you need to know before you make a decision.

The Twenty Questions You Should Ask The Agent

- ❏ How many clients does your agency represent?
- ❏ Is your forte, TV, film, commercials, theater or do you cover actors across the board?
- ❏ Do you develop new talent and how do you go about it?
- ❏ How often should I expect to go on auditions?
- ❏ Do you have established relationships with many casting directors and studios?
- ❏ Who are some of your working clients?
- ❏ How do you see marketing me?
- ❏ Are you SAG franchised?
- ❏ Is your agency's emphasis adults or children?
- ❏ What are you looking for in new talent?
- ❏ How many new clients do you take on each year?
- ❏ How many agents are in your company?
- ❏ Do you do follow-ups after auditions?
- ❏ Do you think my present headshot is effective?
- ❏ What classes in town do you recommend?
- ❏ Do you attend showcases?
- ❏ How do you see my casting?
- ❏ Do you work with managers?
- ❏ Would you represent me across the board? i.e. theater, film, tv, commercials?
- ❏ Do you usually obtain actor interviews through picture submissions or established relationships?

Practical Advice:

Please bear in mind that these are very direct question, which your interviewer might find uncomfortable and might not want to answer. They may hedge their response or say something you don't want to hear. Therefore, it is unwise to put them on the defensive; understand to whom you are talking. Pose your inquires with tact and in a way that makes them feel you are inquisitive and interested. Do not challenge them, causing them to feel they must prove themselves. So go in, have fun, ask intelligent questions, but don't be over zealous and make them feel like you are an archbishop of the Spanish Inquisition.

PEOPLE AND COMPANIES YOU MAILED TO THIS MONTH

Xerox the following pages and make sure to keep an accurate record of all you auditions both for tax purposes and personal growth. Save all related receipts!

Company:
Person:
Phone:
Address:
Date:
Response:

Company:
Person:
Phone:
Address:
Date:
Response:

Company:
Person:
Phone:
Address:
Date:
Response:

Company:
Person:
Phone:
Address:
Date:
Response:

Company:
Person:
Phone:
Address:
Date:
Response:

Company:
Person:
Phone:
Address:
Date:
Response:

CHAPTER 9

Step Nine, Month Nine

Preparing For The First Audition

> "Auditioning is like playing the lottery. And like gambling, it's addictive. You always think, 'Next time I'm gonna hit the jackpot and land that starring role.'"
> —April Lerman, **Charles in Charge**

> "Auditions are your best friends. They give you the opportunity to get jobs, recognition, and pay your rent. Treat them well."
> —Shelly Desai, **award winning TV and stage actor**

The time, work and preparation put forth, thus far, have all been building blocks for this step. **Auditioning**. This is why you have made the move to LA—to pursue a professional acting career. Auditioning is an art form all unto itself that some actors find to be as natural as breathing while others see it as an unnatural event, difficult to learn, and harder to master. For these type of people, the audition becomes a major obstacle. Auditioning can consume you with trepidation and doubt. It becomes *the* major event of the week, rather than being a part of the day. At the audition, you are the director, producer and star! Everything is in your hands, so relish the moment and make the best of it.

Extremes in reality are never black and white. It all comes down to an actor's ability to prepare properly and handle obstacles that impede success. Everyone feels nervous auditioning. Everyone has his or her moment of doubt and fear. Whoever tells you they don't is either lying or doesn't care about what they are doing.

Being prepared does not only mean knowing your lines. It also means being prepared emotionally, professionally and physically. It also means being confident in yourself and not letting the negative voices of doubt sabotage your career. When you walk in the room, stay focused on what you have to do; don't compare yourself to the other actors in the room. You have the ability and the talent.

Timing

Are you on time? This may sound like common knowledge, but it is imperative. You would be surprised how many times actors forget or lose their chance by showing up late or not at all. Tardiness reflects poorly on you, your agent, and your manager. Rescheduling is not an event that your agent and the casting director want to do. It's difficult enough to set up appointments. This is LA and traffic is unpredictable. So please leave plenty of time for driving. It is Murphy's Law concerning LA; if you are rushing, there will be some toxic airborne event that will block the roads in every direction.

Preparation

Make sure before you leave the house, you review this checklist for everything you may need for the audition.

- Directions
- Headshot and resume
- Address
- *Thomas Guide*
- Cell Phone or a pocket full of quarters
- Beeper
- Script or sides
- Highlighter and pen
- Make-up and hair brush
- Phone book with your agent's and manager's phone numbers as well as the casting office you are going to
- A change of clothes, if necessary
- Breath mints
- A bottle of water in case you get dry mouth just before going in
- Lip balm if your lips tend to get dry and crack
- Money for parking
- Confidence

Every audition is different, depending on the medium, i.e. film, TV commercials, half hour comedies, hour shows or theater. The common denominator is it in the audition and your need to be prepared for whatever gets thrown at you. whether it is a prepared reading from a script, a cue card, a cold reading, or an improvisation. Preparation does not mean lack of spontaneity. It is important to follow directions—absolutely imperative. Show your talent within the confines of the directions you are given. Being an actor and giving a great audition does not mean going crazy. Beginning actors often confuse acting wild with talent. Seasoned actors find freedom within the appropriate boundaries.

Here are a few ideas to mull over in your mind as you enter the casting office. Some people use these questions to motivate their reading. Keep these in the back of your brain so that if the casting director throws you a curve, you've got it all covered.

- What role you are auditioning for?
- Whom you are auditioning for?
- What genre is the piece?
- Is it a comedy or drama?
- Is it a one-hour drama?
- Is it a sitcom?
- Is it a reoccurring part?
- Is it a replacement role?
- Is it a principal part?
- Is it an under five?
- What does your character dress like? (You do not need to dress like a filthy bum if that's the role, but do not go in a tuxedo either; dress something close to character, but you do not need to go to a costume place to get a full costume.)
- Where does your character come from?
- Do they have an accent?
- Is it an independent film?
- Is it a studio film?
- Is there a budget?

If you are unsure about any of these questions, ask your agent or manager. It is their job to provide you with as much information as possible. If feasible, try to get the sides the night before the audition, (unless it is a commercial). This way you have plenty of time to get familiar with the character and the lines.

The Audition

When you arrive, sign your name on the call sheet and then take a couple of moments to review the sides. Warm up, using your own personal techniques or the exercises you have learned in class. It is also a good idea to find someone who is reading for the same project but a different part to run lines with. Different actors will give you different interpretations. This will help you avoid being stuck in a fixed line reading. It is better to allow extra time to prepare. You do not want to appear rushed and disheveled. You can never be too prepared, so stay focused-and avoid a lot of chit-chat with the other actors. Above all, R-E-L-A-X. When you enter the casting room, keep the "hellos," to a minimum. Be cordial, but stay with what you have to do. When you enter the room, read the room; this means quickly assessing the mood in the room. Some rooms are warmer (emotionally in ambiance) than others. Some people watching your audition are gregarious, funny, etc.; others may be reserved and distant. Note: If there are more than two people in the room, do not shake everyone's hand. After the audition, leave; do not linger.

No matter what type of audition you are going for, there are certain tips that are universal. Before you enter the room where you are auditioning, make strong character choices and believe you have as good of a shot as any of the other actors at booking the job.

Commercials

If it is a commercial audition, they will have you slate your name before you read anything—do not blow this off or minimize this. Sometimes the slate is all they see when they scan through the hours of casting tapes that the day. Slate with a warm inviting smile. Clearly state your name and your agency. If you wear glasses (not sun glasses), ask to slate both with and without them. After you slate your name, do not be scared to take a couple of moments to get into character, even if the camera is still running. It's your time; take charge.

Most commercial auditions have cue cards since you only receive the script when you arrive. At the audition there is little time for memorization. While this might sound easy, reading cue cards takes practice. You need to train your eyes not to focus on the cue cards but to make contact with the camera. This can be a tricky skill to master because the cue card is placed so close to the actual camera. You never want to look as you if you are reading. Convey your story, love what you are selling, but never come off like a used car salesman. Make strong character choices, and when you look at the camera, know whom you are talking to. Is this your child? your boss? your spouse or your best friend? You have to be imaginative in commercial auditions because commercial scripts can have limited information.

According to actor Billy Jayne, who can be seen several times a day on numerous national commercials, "The key to nailing a commercial audition is connect to the character you choose to portray and make bold choices. When I am auditioning, nothing else exists, except living truthfully in that moment. I do not act as if I am auditioning for that job. I become the character. I live the situation for the length of time the camera is rolling. I am not looking for anyone's approval or acceptance. I walk, talk, move and dress like the character. I know the character's history, his family and what kind of day he had. When they say cut, I do not judge or critique my own performance When they say cut, I thank them and leave. I am booking, so I guess I am doing something right."

Auditioning For Film

Films cost a lot more than TV; an average studio film costs forty million. Therefore, more time and care are taken in casting. You may get to read the whole script, not just your part or the sides. You may even get the script an entire week in advance or at least a few days before the audition.

Since they are spending all this money, they expect you not only to play the part well but bring something special or memorable to the role; for example, a certain behavior or perhaps some unexpected humor or speech pattern etc.

You may be videotaped or you may be doing it live in front of the director, producer, and casting director—sometimes even the film's star.

In the room, arrange, within reason, the furniture, etc., the way you see the scene. Do not mess up somebody's desk. Do not bring a weapon, but certainly use a suitable substitute, if you must; for example, a pencil for a knife. Dress something like the part, but do not buy a new wardrobe. They are watching what is happening with your face and eyes and body. The camera catches you—and it's relentless—it never blinks. They do not care about your clothes. Remember, in films the close up is everything. One great close up is better than a lot of screen time when you are ten or fifteen feet from the camera. When you watch movies, watch the close ups. That's the "money" in movies. Make sure you make real eye contact with your partner even if he/she is just a reader. Not just fleeting glances but real eye contact—something that conveys something-this does not mean stare.

Practical Film Auditioning Tips

- *Keep the script at a reasonable distance from your face, preferably to the side—left or right—so the camera can see you.*
- *Even if you have memorized the script, carry it and hold the sides as if you haven't*
- *Memorizing is not necessary especially if it causes anxiety and takes away from your performance*
- *Lines are not that critical in an audition. What they want to see is your take on the role, your imagination, and how you fulfill it.*

Practical Stage Auditioning Tips

Theater is the most difficult venue, because there are no retakes; it's live. They are looking at how well you project your voice and facial features. They want to make sure you can improvise if thrown a curve while performing. They want a consummate professional.

- *Know as much of the play as possible, not just your speech or scene.*
- *Do it your way (how you see the role), but be prepared to try other options, (either your own or with direction) this is so you can pick up traits about your scene that may not be apparent.*
- *Do it full out without holding back, but do not physically hurt anyone or destroy furniture.*
- *If it is a small room watch your volume.*
- *Usually there is a reader; connect with him or her as much as possible. This is very important—a lot more than the lines.*
- *Above all, do not let them see you sweat, unless you are playing a sweaty guy or girl!*
- *In theater as opposed to commercials, film, and TV, vocal ability is one of the most important things (that is being able to project to the last row)*
- *So train your voice to project without shouting—classes, classes, classes are imperative! (Refer back to step four).*

Additional Thoughts

Of course, it is important to know who you are as person—for everyone-but especially for an actor. How you arrive at that is dealt with in previous chapters. As an actor, it is important how other people perceive you. There is the story of the actor who went to the airport to ask ten strangers what they thought of him! If this rings a bell, you need to work on your person before you seriously start auditioning. For the rest of you, you're on your way!!

Twenty Questions You Should Ask Yourself Before Going On An Audition

❑ Do you have the name of the person or people you are seeing?

❑ Do you have the correct address and directions to get to the audition?

❑ Do you know the role and the pages you need to prepare?

❑ How are you getting the material, i.e. faxed from the production office, or are you picking it up?

❑ Do I have a method of preparing, i.e. voice, stretching, meditation, etc.?

❑ What are the specifics they are looking for, i.e. dialect, dress, a certain character interpretation?

❑ Have you reviewed the material, so you are very familiar with the character and scene?

❑ Have you run the lines with somebody, i.e. friends, family, teachers?

❑ Do you know the director's body of work?

❑ Is the part a featured role, under five, guest star, co-star or just a featured extra?

❑ If this is a television series, have you seen the show? Do you know who the stars are? Do you know what network producers it? Do you know if this is a sit-com, drama or a movie of the week?

❑ Do you know how to present yourself professionally when you walk in the casting office, i.e. knowing not to chit-chat, getting right to work, staying focused?

❑ Is this is a low budget film or an independent project, or are there any established name actors attached? Is this a student film from USC, AFI, UCLA? If this is a major feature film, is it studio backed or distributed and who are the stars of the project?

❑ Do you have your agent's numbers with you

❑ Do you have your picture and resume with you?

❑ Have you done all the emotional work needed to give a great audition?

❑ Do you have change for the parking meter?

❑ Is it a period piece? Does it require an accent?

❑ Do you have a bottle of water so you don't get dehydrated?

❑ Are you ready to knock them dead?

Xerox the following pages and make sure to keep an accurate record of all you auditions both for tax purposes and personal growth. Save all related receipts!

Audition Record
PROJECT: DATE:

PRODUCTION

Role:

Film ? Television ? Theater ? Commercial ? Other:

Director: Production Company:

Other Actors Involved:

Union ?   Non Union ?   Shooting Schedule:

CASTING COMPANY

Casting Director:
Assistant:
Address   Phone:

Pick Up Sides At:

Special Notes:

AUDITION

Time:
Wardrobe:
My Choices:
Self Evaluation:

NOTES

Audition Record
PROJECT: **DATE:**

PRODUCTION

Role:

Film ? Television ? Theater ? Commercial ? Other:

Director: Production Company:

Other Actors Involved:

Union ?   Non Union ?   Shooting Schedule:

CASTING COMPANY

Casting Director:
Assistant:
Address   Phone:

Pick Up Sides At:

Special Notes:

AUDITION

Time:
Wardrobe:
My Choices:
Self Evaluation:

NOTES

What Can I Improve Upon Next Month And The Months To Come?

**Inspiring Comments Or
Compliments I Have Received:**

_____
_____
_____
_____
_____
_____
_____
_____
_____
_____
_____
_____
_____
_____
_____
_____
_____
_____
_____
_____
_____
_____
_____
_____
_____
_____
_____
_____
_____
_____
_____
_____
_____
_____
_____

People Or Actors Who Have Inspired Me Professionally:

Affirmations :

1. I Am Special
2. I Am Gifted
3. I Am Unique
4. I Deserve Success
5.
6.
7.
8.
9.
10.
11.
12.
13.
14.
15.
16.
17.
18.
19.
20.

Make Sure To Look At These Daily

Dreams

 **Write Yourself A Rave Review**

What Did You Do?

How Did You Put Your Unique Signature On it?

Make Sure It Includes How Wonderful You Are.
This is for you and you only to remind yourself how special you are, even on the tough days.

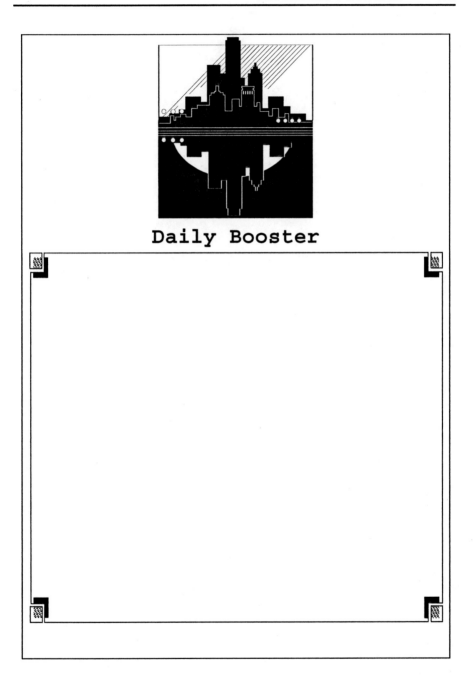

Daily Booster

CHAPTER 10

Step Ten, Month Ten

Yes! I Have A Callback!

"During the callback we are looking for the actor to breathe life into the character…bring something fresh and novel that will make us stand up and take notice after seeing the material performed a hundred times."
—Debi Manwiller
Casting Director, *Chicago Hope* and *LA Doctors*

You are now in a possible position to book the job. Having a call back, regardless of the outcome, will not necessarily make or break your career. Of course, it is inevitable that you will meet actors, who, for whatever reason, are fortunate enough to secure many call-backs. They seem to have luck, looks, and even charisma on their side. You look at them and wonder, "What do they have that I don't? Why are their experiences with call-backs different than mine? How do they lock down the job?" Unfortunately, there are no definitive answers. Everyone is different and every actor, in spite of his success or lack of it, is different.

Some actors rehearse their scenes as many times as possible in order to present something polished and exact. Other actors review the material, make a few additional choices that seem appropriate and then put the script/ sides away, so as not to become stale and predictable. The other approach an actor takes is to leave his audition up to instinct and impulse. This last process is obviously not our suggested method of choice. It provides the actor with an excuse not to prepare and prevents him from learning how to perfect his craft and nail the call back, thus booking the job.

When it comes down to it, the actor needs to give a performance with a beginning, middle, and end even when they have their script/ sides in hand. They need to create a character, communicate with their partner, and have a point of view that expresses who they are. All of which is based on the actor's ability to understand the scene, which then reveals their artistic choices. The ultimate goal for this step is to secure the job at hand.

Beginners—even seasoned professionals—feel a certain degree of pressure during this phase of the casting process; it is only natural. Actors want to do the best job they can. They want to be acknowledged. They also want people to recognize their talent; but most importantly, they want to *get hired and get a paycheck.* However, the actor needs to learn how to overcome the pressures. Regardless of experience, it is your responsibility to book this job.

For the new actor, the call back should be seen not only as an opportunity to attain work, but also as a venue to meet and establish yourself with professionals. The pressure you feel during the audition, the need to get the job, is also due in part to your excitement, and also your sheer desire to work. The tension you suddenly experience should take a back seat to those feelings that allow you to be more available and creative. Do your best to get rid of the tension while you are in the room. It kills everything. Tension is your enemy!

This does not mean you should approach the audition as though you have no chance of being hired because of your lack of experience. Neither should you feel the call back is a fluke. The attitude you carry into the room also determines your level of professionalism and success. Your attitude is perhaps the most important thing; it may either help you or hinder you._

In addition, the number of times you are called back, even the type of notes you are asked to incorporate into your next reading, always varies according to the project and the people involved. Moreover, the medium for which the script is being produced, whether it's film, television or theater, also determines the style and temperament of the audition.

However, some call backs, regardless of the medium, are not able to provide the actor and director with the opportunity to develop a connection or work on the scene(s) in depth. The actor is called into a room, where sitting in front of him are the casting people, the director, and at least two or more of the producers. These individuals have been waiting to see your work. They also want you to be the actor who makes an entrance, exudes confidence, and give the performance they envision.

"If you don't make an impression on me, you certainly won't make one on an audience that I care about"—Jeremy Goldscheider, Commercial Director The decision to hire or pass on a particular actor is made very quickly. The actor comes in, says hello, may ask a question or two, but then has to give a riveting performance.

The casting process in television is very fast. Hour and half-hour programs, which are respectfully called episodics and sitcoms, hire every week to fill guest starring roles and day player roles. This puts actors in the position of needing to be prepared at a moment's notice to return for a callback and to read for the producer and director. Therefore, do not throw away the sides after the initial audition. You never know when your luck will hit. Do not leave town unexpectedly without consulting your agent.

Other call-backs, such as film and stage interviews, are totally different experiences. The rush to get in and out is now replaced with an opportunity for the director and actor to exchange ideas and concepts about the character and the script. Both parties have time to do the following:

- Learn more about the person(s) sitting in front of them and if they can work together.
- Can the actor execute the director's notes quickly?
- Does the actor fulfill the director's conception of the role? Is this how the part should be played?
- If not, can the actor change the Director's vision, thereby putting the actor in serious contention for the role?
- Does the actor give a performance that tells everyone in the room that this in how the part should be played?

Do not change anything from your first audition—the first time you read for the part. That means wear the same outfit, do not get a hair-cut, do not spend excessive amounts of time in the sun, or change your hair color. Maintain the same attitude you had going in for the casting director and stay with the choices you made the first time around. Memorization is not always necessary. Sometimes that leads the beginning or even trained actor into worrying about lines. They begin giving line readings rather than reacting in the moment unless you are an exception and can give a fresh and new performance each time.

On a call back, it is not necessary to shake hands with everyone in the room. Making contact, looking at each person, and acknowledging them is fine. The most important thing to remember is that you are there to do a job, not socialize. Excessive conversation, or trying to be funny or general socializing detracts from who are. It's times like this when the actor can lose the job before he reads the first line. An actor is hired for his ability, but is also hired because the director and producer can talk to and work with them for the next couple weeks or so.

Do not bring anything into the audition that may be threatening to the people in the office. People are very nervous about individuals losing control; so if the scene calls for a gun or knife, use your finger, or pretend you are holding the knife in your hand. What's important is what you do, the choices you make, and the emotional connection to the material. Often your body says more than the words. Eye contact is very important.

Above all, it's something intangible that happens between you, the producer, and the director that gets you the job. That is why you need to be prepared when you walk in the office—in order to allow that special moment to happen organically. But in the end, none of this is important if you do not enjoy yourself and have fun. The last thing you want to do is project the feeling that this is an excruciatingly painful moment and that you would rather have root canal than be with them.

However, if you are a golf or tennis buddy to the producer, then all of the above is mute. You secure the job on the golf course—no audition, no interview.

Lastly, when you finish the reading, **leave,** do not hang around and chit chat. Actors can have the job one minute then, literally, talk themselves out of the part the next. Don't degrade your work at the end by asking if what you did was okay or good. Don't plant something in their minds which may convince them their instincts were wrong. They are just as nervous as you; your job is to make them secure with casting you!

Twenty Questions To Ask Yourself Before You Go On The Call Back

❑   Am I wearing the outfit I wore at the first audition?

❑   Does my hair closely resemble what it was when they first met me?

❑   Do I have a tan or sunburn that wasn't there a day or a week ago? If so, you may have to use the appropriate make-up to darken or lighten as needed.

❑   Do I know where I am going?

❑   Do I have the script or sides from the script with me?

❑   Have I prepared enough so I am familiar with the character and scene?

❑   Do I have my picture and resume?

❑   Do I know who is going to be in the room when I audition?

❑   Do I have gas in my car?

❑   Do I have the number of the casting office in the event I get lost or am late so I can inform them of my whereabouts?

❑   Do I have money to park the car in a lot or on the street if there is no side street parking?

❑   Am I giving myself enough time to get to the appointment without rushing and on the way get in an accident?

❑   If you need to have the gym as part of your daily routine, make sure it's scheduled accordingly—as well as any other physical or vocal work that you might want to do.

❑ How is your hygiene? Do you have to use any breath spay before you go in. Do not smoke before you walk in the room. Do not cover it up with too much cologne or perfume. All these smells and odors can be offensive and turn them off to you.

❑ Do you know what time it is and how long it's going to take you to get to your destination?

❑ If you tend to have low blood sugar, have you eaten or are you bringing something with you to snack on?

❑ Do you have your purse, knapsack, etc. for touchups if you are a girl? If you are a guy, the bathroom towels will do just fine

❑ Do you need to have water or a soft drink before you go in so as not to have dry mouth? Remember Los Angeles resides on the outskirts of the desert and it gets very dry and hot.

❑ If you are away from your home, have you checked your messages to see if there have been any changes in the time or place for your audition?

❑ Do not carry any negativity or upset in your life or other people's lives into the audition. Leave your personal problem outside the door. Go in have fun and book the job.

Practical Note: The following audition records and tax sheets are important to save in case you ever get audited.

As a working actor, many of your purchases including study materials, equipment, transportation, props, and audition material are tax deductible. So try to keep accurate logs of your purchases, and do not wait to the end of the year to organize your receipts.

Keep all of the receipts that are related to your career in itemized envelopes. Unfortunately, unless you earn money in the entertainment field, you can't deduct any of your expenses!

Unless you are making money, the government will consider your acting a hobby. Remember, costumes not every day clothes are tax deductible. If you can wear them as street clothes, the IRS will rule out the deduction. The following list is a guideline. Use it! You and your accountant will thank us when tax time comes around.

No Nonsense TAX WORK SHEET

Name _____

Tax Deductions

Accompanists		Tele-biz use	
Agent/Mgr Fees		Trade Pubs	
Auto/biz use		Utilities-biz	
Backstage Tips		Tvl-Lodging	
Cable TV		Tvl-Meals	
Coaching/Dance		Tvl-Air fares	
Coaching/Drama		Tvl-Auto Rental	
Coaching/Music		Tvl-Park & Toll	
Costumes		Tvl-Local Trans	
Dues/Union		Tvl-Laundry	
Entertainment		Tvl-ServiceTips	
Gifts-biz		Tvl-Luggage	
Hair Care-biz			
Insurance-biz			
Legal/Accounting			
Local Transportation			
Make-up/Wigs			
Office Supplies		Medical Insurance	
Postage		Doctors, etc	
Printing/Copy		Tvl to Dr.	
Piano Tuning		Real Estate Tax	
Equipment		Mortg Points	
Equipment Repair		Mortg Interest	
Tickets			
Photos		Charity	
Studio Rental			
Study Material		IRA Contribution	
Supplies			
Tel Ans Svc		College tuition	
Tel-Long Dist		College rm & bd	

❑ If any IRS or state estimated payments, list dates and amount of <u>each</u> payment on back of Summary Information sheet.

❑ If any capital gains sales, give <u>date acquired</u> and <u>cost</u> of asset on back of Summary Information sheet.

Xerox the following pages and make sure to keep an accurate record of all you callbacks both for tax purposes and personal growth. Save all related receipts!

Callback Record	
PROJECT:	**DATE:**

PRODUCTION

Role:

Film ? Television ? Theater ? Commercial ? Other:

Director: Production Company:

Other Actors Involved:

Union ?   Non Union ?   Shooting Schedule:

CASTING COMPANY

Casting Director:
Assistant:
Address   Phone:

Pick Up Sides At:

Special Notes:

CALLBACK

Time:
Wardrobe:
My Choices:
Self Evaluation:

NOTES

Callback Record
PROJECT: **DATE:**

PRODUCTION

Role:

Film ? Television ? Theater ? Commercial ? Other:

Director: Production Company:

Other Actors Involved:

Union ?   Non Union ?   Shooting Schedule:

CASTING COMPANY

Casting Director:
Assistant:
Address   Phone:

Pick Up Sides At:

Special Notes:

CALLBACK

Time:
Wardrobe:
My Choices:
Self Evaluation:

NOTES

Callback Record

PROJECT: **DATE:**

PRODUCTION

Role:

Film ? Television ? Theater ? Commercial ? Other:

Director: Production Company:

Other Actors Involved:

Union ?   Non Union ?   Shooting Schedule:

CASTING COMPANY

Casting Director:
Assistant:
Address   Phone:

Pick Up Sides At:

Special Notes:

CALLBACK

Time:
Wardrobe:
My Choices:
Self Evaluation:

NOTES

CHAPTER 11

Step Eleven, Month Eleven

Expanding your community

> Actors must create a "buzz" about themselves by getting seen. Some actors perform in plays, showcases, even create their own independent films...other do stand-up comedy.
>
> —Aaron Priceman
> Sitcom Actor

Gaining exposure through theater companies, independent films, showcases and readings are excellent ways to expand your network, meet new people, hone your craft and gain needed exposure. Contrary to many New Yorker's opinions—who believe there is no theater only film in LA, a snooty misconception—there is good theater outside New York. Theater helps the actor remain in shape as well as providing a public venue in which to be seen. LA is filled with many excellent theaters and theater companies.

The theater community may seem elitist; however, once you get involved it becomes a much less transient and much safer place than the film world. It's a place where actors, writers, and directors come together and practice, develop, and stage both new and established works.

There are several theater companies in LA that either welcome new members through auditions or take apprentices (actors who don't have enough professional acting credits on their resume to be considered for membership, but can work their way up to membership by going through an apprentice program). An apprentice usually has to donate time working backstage in order to pay his dues. It's similar to pledging a fraternity or sorority. Only the stage is not as cruel. The pledging process at a reputable company should not be torturous; rather it should be a positive learning experience.

DAWN

After a couple of months of living in LA, I was fortunate enough to be accepted into a reputable apprentice program at a company called Theater East—

located above Jerry's Deli in Studio City. (Try the corned beef.) It was here that I felt most at home in LA. The apprentice program was very regimented and time consuming, but it was well worth it. At Theater East, I participated in readings showcases and performances, but I also created lasting friendships, learned how to launch my own projects and gained support. On a social level, I found lasting friends, interesting part time jobs, and great housing situations. I experienced and learned about the business of acting, hands on! Moreover, I gained exposure to working professionals in all areas of the business that paid off in ways I never would have imagined.

Agent representation, auditions and learning how to produce were not my motivation for joining the company or something I even imagined—but it was some of the benefits. The Theatre East roster of members included: reputable casting directors, agents, film and TV directors and producers. It was an exciting safe environment to make connections and work on character parts that perhaps were not my casting in the real world, but were allowed in this venue. Every theater company is different, and again you have to find a group that suits your particular needs or if you are a driven, make it happen type of person, you could create your own company.

Because the theater world is tenuous, financially small companies come and go faster then SBC can list them in the yellow pages. This is not to discourage you from starting up something of your own. However, all you really need is space, which is relative…I've rehearsed and performed in public parks…and some good writing. If you have a script you want produced, you should go for it no matter what. Creativity is contagious and good writing is always hard to find, as you will see when you begin working in LA or anywhere else. Just because an already established theater house can't recognize the brilliance that lies in your script, that doesn't mean you shouldn't be able to perform or produce it. "A producer is only as good as his script."

This can be applied to the performer as well. Gather a group of actors that you trust and would like to work with, as well as with a few hundred dollars, you can incorporate and start making theater. It's that easy and you will have a venue to showcase your talent and all the professional strides you've made in the last eleven months. The hard part is staying alive…translation…making a living doing it.

This also applies to doing an independent film. What you need is a good script, some talented actors, some basic crew people (i.e. cameraman, lighting man, director, enthusiasm) and a bit of money that you can either raise or max out on your credit cards. Guerrilla filmmaking is arduous work, but the rewards can be great. Just ask Spike Lee or Edward Burns.

As a young actress working a double shift at Jerry's Deli, I became disheartened as I began talking with a fellow waitress on my all night shift, who was not exactly an ingénue. She had been struggling as an actress for more than fifty years. She was still very into her "career." She bragged about all the people she met waiting tables in the last fifty years. She believed her big break was coming soon. I became depressed listening to her optimism. I was not about to wait 50 years, let alone 50 minutes. That night I went home and decided I was going to form my own production company. It was during this moment of clarity that I decided I was not going to be passive in my career choices. Thus was born Grinning Gorilla Films.

I produced several shorts and commercials by pulling out my Rolodex of business cards which I acquired after living my first year in LA. This is not to say it was an easy task or a job for anyone. You need to have a certain personality. I have always believed that you create your own destiny. Hollywood is not a friendly town. More often than not, you have to create your own creative environment to give yourself and your work a chance.

If you feel more comfortable utilizing conventional methods, listed below is a compilation of established theater companies and networking "hot tips." But if you don't discourage easily, I am a huge advocate for self starting. This way you are a participant in your creative destiny rather than just a passenger going along for the ride. Fill out the worksheets at the end chapter to help you define the type of actor you are.

Theater Companies We Really Like

The Actors Gang
6209 Santa Monica Blvd.
Hollywood CA
(323) 465-0566

The Actors Studio
8341 De long pre Ave
West Hollywood CA
(323) 654-7125
A world renowned company. You can be accepted after two auditions—the first is a primary; the second is a final

Circus Theatricals
2055 S. Sepulveda Blvd.
(310) 226-6144
Must audition, there are monthly dues.

Classical Theater Lab
At Hollywood Court Theater
6817 Highland Avenue, Hollywood
(323) 960-5691
Must audition. Quarterly dues.

Colony Theater Company
555 North 3rd Street, Burbank
(818) 558-7000
Very Prestigious Paying company.

Company of Angels
2106 Hyperion Ave.
Silverlake, CA
(323) 883-1717
Auditions are required.

East West Players
120 Judge John Aiso
LA, CA
(213) 625-7000
There is an emphasis on Asian American plays and talent.

Interact theater Company
5215 Bakman Street
NoHo, CA
(818) 765-8732
Auditions are a must and tuitions due monthly.

Lankersheim Arts Center—The Road Theater
5108 Lankersheim Blvd.-(NoHo)
LA CA
(818)761-8838
Monday night readings-series (free)

A Noise Within
234 S. Brand Blvd.
Glendale, CA
(818) 240-0910
Open auditions for accomplished actors.

Sacred Fools Theater Company
660 Heliotrope drive
(323) 666-506
Innovative theater. Bold and experimental. Just show up for meetings. No auditions required.

Theater East—
12655 Ventura Blvd.
(818) 760-4160
Founded in 1960; located above Jerry's Deli in Studio City
Apprenticeships available

Theater 40
241 Marino Drive
Beverly Hills, CA
(310) 364-0535

Theater West
3333 Cahuenga Blvd.
Hollywood, CA
(323) 851-4839
A membership company of actors, directors, and writers.

Great Places to Network

Actor's Network
12455 Moore Park, Studio City
(818) 509-1010
For professional actors, many guest speakers.

Coffee Bean
Sunset Plaza
8591 Sunset Blvd., West Hollywood
(310) 659-1890

Film Makers Alliance
453 South Spring
(213) 228-1152
A networking and support group for independent filmmakers, actors and directors.
Yearly dues.

First Stage
6817 Franklin Blvd., HWD
(323) 850-6271
Dedicated to new material for stage and screen. Actors needed for Monday night readings.

IFP
8750 Wilshire Blvd., B. H.
Beverly Hills, CA
(310) 432-1200
$85 a year entitles you to independent film screenings, lectures and many resources.

Improv
8162 Melrose Avenue
(323) 651-2583
Mo-Betta-Monday

African and Hispanic comics. Always crowded.

In The Act
10015 Venice Blvd., LA
(310) 281-7772
Workshops with known casting directors. Auditions required for acceptance

Jerry's Famous Deli—open 24 hours
12655 Ventura Blvd., Studio City
(818) 980-4245
Theater East is located upstairs and the actors usually meet afterwards. A casual meeting place for actors

One On One
13261 Moorpark, Sherman Oaks
(818) 789-3399
Cold reading workshops. Private instructors. Meet big casting directors. Must audition.

Reel Pros
13437 Ventura Blvd., Sherman Oaks
(818) 788-4133
Casting Director workshops. Stringent auditions.

Silver Spoon Restaurant
8171 Santa Monica Blvd., W. HWD
(323) 650-4890
Actors usually meet Friday afternoons from 1:00 pm–4:00 pm. However the age range usually varies.

Take One—Film & Theatre Bookstore
1156 Santa Monica Blvd, West LA
(310) 445-4050
Industry lecture series.

TVI
14429 Ventura Blvd., Sherman Oaks
(818) 784-6500
Learning how to get the job done.
Taught by casting directors.

Urth Cafe
8565 Melrose Ave., W. HWD
(310) 659-0628
Great for coffee, people watching &
networking

Women in Film
8857 West Olympic Blvd., B. H.
(310) 657-6144

Women in Theater
11684 Ventura Blvd., Studio City
(818) 763-5222
Empowering women in the performing arts through performance,
education and networking.

On-line Networking-Services-Directory

Academy Player Directory www.playersdirectory.com *1313 North Vine Street, Hollywood* *(310) 247-3058* Must be a member of an actors union to be listed. **Acting Zone** http://actingzone.com/ casting and contact information for performers from LA to NY. **AWOL** Actors workshop on-line http://www.redbirdstudio.com/AWOL/acting2.html Great for industry articles and local castings.	**Cast Net** *(323)964-4900* www.castnet.com on line submissions free for union members **LA Casting.com** *6671 Sunset Blvd., Hollywood* *(323) 462-8200* Theatrical and commercials. Actor's pictures and resumes are on the net for casting directors to access. Free for members with agent representation. **Showfax** www.showfax.com *2140 Cotner, West LA* *(310) 385-6920* Yearly fee or pay by the page. Will fax sides or send them overnight.

Twenty Questions You Should Ask Yourself To Make Sure You Are Getting Yourself Out There And Networking.

❑ Have you looked into all the theater companies that are casting or looking for members in Los Angeles?

❑ Have you joined or started a support group?

❑ Have you developed relationships with the people in your acting class where you discuss what is going on around town?

❑ Have you joined an acting class?

❑ Do you go to theater in LA?

❑ Do you go to showcases to see who else is out there?

❑ Are you putting together a showcase for yourself?

❑ Are you auditioning for showcases at reputable schools?

❑ Have you met any industry professionals through your networking?

❑ Do you maintain communication after you say you will call them?

❑ Do you follow up or just keep in touch on a regular basis?

❑ Do you get people to see your work whenever you are performing in something?

❑ Do you know people you can call, who know and enjoy your work, and who are in a position to make a call to someone in the business who can hire you and get you working?

❑ Do you put on a show when you talk to people or are you just yourself?

❑ Do you come across as someone people want to help or do they see you as unapproachable and arrogant?

❑ Have you thought about writing your own material to showcase your talents?

❑ Do you send out photos and resumes to agents and managers and post cards to casting directors?

❑ Are there directors you would like to work with? If so, find their address, their agent, their production company, and constantly write them?

❑ Do you go to discussions or meeting where actors, directors and writers are, i.e. AFI or the Independent Film Project West?

❑ If you know of these sessions, have you joined them and are going regularly?

PLACES I WENT TO NETWORK THIS MONTH

Places	People	Phone	Comments

Worksheet

Pro's and Con's of Starting Your Own Company
(Answer these questions honestly to see if you are the self-starting type)

Do I have material that I would really like to see produced? What is it?

_____

_____

Are other talented and dedicated actors willing to go into this venture with me? Who?

_____

_____

Do I have access to some money to get the proverbial ball rolling? How much?

_____

_____

Do I have the amount of time and energy necessary?

_____

_____

How badly do I want this to happen? Is this ego driven or true dedication and passion?

_____

_____

How well do I handle obstacles, red tape and rejection?

_____

_____

Am I able to take-charge and delegate authority?

_____

_____

Do I have good communication skills?

_____

_____

List three words that you would use to describe yourself

1. _____
2. _____
3. _____

Use three words that others would use to describe you.

1. _____
2. _____
3. _____

What are my three greatest strengths?

1. _____
2. _____
3. _____

What are my three greatest weaknesses?

1. _____
2. _____
3. _____

Are my strengths and weaknesses compatible with being a leader?

PRO'S

_____

_____

_____

_____

_____

_____

_____

_____

_____

CON'S

_____

_____

_____

_____

_____

_____

_____

_____

CHAPTER 12

Step Twelve, Month Twelve

YOU GOT THE JOB!! A DREAM COME TRUE

> You never know how high you can reach until you are called to rise.
> —Emily Dickinson

Congratulations!! The day you've been waiting for has arrived, working as a professional actor. There is no feeling of satisfaction as wonderful as this. It's truly a high. But now you need to work in overdrive. You want to appear calm, prepared, and professional arriving to work. You need to know what to do, where to go, how to conduct yourself as well as being aware of union rules and entitlements. Each job varies depending on the medium your working in, i.e. stage, TV or film.

Mostly likely the person who informed you that you booked the job is your agent or manager. After you let out a deep guttural scream of happiness sounding similar to childbirth, compose yourself and take down all the appropriate information in your calendar or notebook. One thing everyone hates in the business is when you call back and ask him or her to repeat everything a second time. This is your career; you are your business. Treat yourself accordingly and with respect. Don't waste people's time by having them do or redo something you should be responsible for anyway. Agents and managers are not your secretary unless you make gazillions of bucks for them. They will help facilitate your career if you don't annoy them.

Nine out of ten times, the *second assistant director* will call you regarding location, times you will be working, as well as new versions of scripts and maps. (Sometimes it's the *production coordinator* who calls instead of the *second assistant director* depending on the size of the production). The *wardrobe assistant* may also call you regarding fittings and sizes.

It is important to know the following:

1. Who are you playing? Sometimes there is a role change.

2. What days are planned for shooting each scene you're in?
3. Are there rehearsal days?
4. Are there travel days? If shooting is being done out of town, how about a per diem (spending cash)?
5. Do the appropriate people from the production company have all your numbers in case of an emergency, including beeper and cell phone?

Location Do's and Don'ts:

The professional is always early and always prepared to do the work that is required of them that day. Being late is not acceptable and reflects poorly on you and your handlers. It is not beyond the production company to call the casting director and complain about the actor for being late. And it's certainly not beyond the producers to fire someone even after a day's work. Getting fired for any reason is possible, it happens all the time. Even being a regular on the show doesn't protect you.

When you get to your location, get a copy of your contract from the production company if you didn't get one from your agent. Make sure you read it! Make certain it corresponds with the information your agent told you! Sometimes a certain negotiation may be "accidentally" omitted. You will also have to fill out two tax forms: an *I-9*, an identification form that you are a citizen and, if not, that you have permission to work and a *W-2*, for federal tax withholdings. You can ask the *2nd AD* for these two items as he will be your contact person for the entire job. He will be the person who will take you to wardrobe, make-up, to your trailer, and then eventually on to the set. Most importantly, don't forget the *time sheet* at the end of the day—this will determine your pay and overtime.

Being serious about your responsibilities will help ensure that this part may lead to another project with the same company or director. So be cool, and relaxed, relish the moment, make some friendships, and plan for future success. Good luck, break a leg, and don't trip over a light.

Little hints they won't tell you at any acting school.

(We are not responsible for the following tricks, they are just rumors that we've found useful.)

- If you have bags under your eyes, put cool tea bags or cucumbers on your eyes.

- If you have pimples, use eye-drops. It gets the red out.

- If you leave the conditioner in your hair longer while in the shower, it won't get frizzy at the end of the day.

- Come with a clean face and hair; don't put on make-up, but bring some just in case.

- Don't eat beans or cheese the night before.

- Don't pig out on the craft service table; there will probably be meals served during the day.

- Eat lightly. The camera adds ten pounds. Some people eat out of boredom—there is a lot of waiting around on sets. Bring a book, knitting anything to occupy your down time. Above all relax, but stay mentally and physically alert and prepared.

Twenty Questions You Should Ask Before You Walk On A Set

❑ Do the appropriate people from the production company have all my numbers in case of an emergency, including beeper and cell phone?

❑ Who is my contact when I get on the set?

❑ Have I prepared myself for the role?

❑ Have I gotten enough rest?

❑ Who am I playing?

❑ Do I know my lines?

❑ Are there any rehearsal days?

❑ How can I center myself if I get major stage fright?

❑ Do I know my call time?

❑ Do I have instructions on how to get to the location?

❑ Do I have money just in case there is an emergency?

❑ Do I have a contact number in case there is a real emergency like a death or accident?

❑ Did I take into account that there may be traffic on the way to set?

❑ If I workout in the morning, did I allow enough time to get in some of my normal routine?

❑ Do I have my sides or script with me?

❑ Did I bring a highlighter and a pen, in case they change the script on me?

❑ Did I bring two forms of ID for my I-9?

❑ Do I have a copy of my picture and resume?

❑ Do have my book to read if I end up waiting around?

❑ How much do I get paid?

One question not to ask the production office on the set; otherwise, they will think you are lazy. Where is the craft service table?

Reflections On My First Year
As An Actor in Los Angeles

Conclusion

Now that you have completed the *Twelve Step Plan To Becoming An Actor In LA* you have the basic building blocks for creating your career as a successful actor in Los Angeles.

You have chosen a path that requires you to have a burn in your heart and a calling to be in the business of acting. This journey will not be easy. There are no quick short cuts. The casting couch will only get you so far. The schmoozing might get you in the door. The headshot will get you noticed. The classes will take you further.

In the end it all comes down to work, work, work—and attitude!! If you have passion, discipline, and focus there will be no stopping you.

Don't wait to be discovered. The old days of Hollywood are gone. Only you can turn your dream into a reality. This book is only a tool for which you can make it come true. Its real value is to empower you to discover yourself!

Without your determination and conscientious attention to you profession, this book will mean nothing except a place to put your coffee.

It is our goal to make you a working actor. We look forward to the day when you will stand in front of the podium on Oscar night accepting an award or see Your face in *Variety.*

Good luck on your wonderful journey...

ABOUT THE AUTHORS

Dawn Lerman began her career as an actress fourteen years ago in Los Angeles. She appeared in several regional theater productions as well as numerous national commercials. This early success led to a meeting with Tony Award-winning playwright George Firth who gave her an opportunity to produce his play, *Precious Sons*. Here she discovered that raising money was one of her many talents. Ms. Lerman went on to produce numerous other stage productions as well as music videos and documentaries. During this time, she worked at Shearson-Lehman-Hutton under the auspices of John Probandt. Her production company Grinning Gorilla Films grew out of this relationship. The company boasted Mazda, Viacom, and AT&T among its many clients. Throughout her career, Ms. Lerman always felt that children needed the assistance of dedicated, passionate people to help them realize their dreams. This belief led her to teach acting to underprivileged youths, which then became the impetus for her going to graduate school at New York University for her Master's in drama therapy. Ms. Lerman continues to bridge her two worlds of psychology and entertainment as she is currently developing an array of children's programming, as well as children's books. Ms. Lerman last worked as a creative arts therapist at the ERAS Center in LA. She is currently on hiatus to raise her her son Dylan Parker Vaccaro.

Dori Keller began his career in the entertainment industry as an actor almost twenty years ago when he entered the four-year professional acting program at the State University of New York at Purchase. His first professional experience started immediately when he appeared for two consecutive years at one this country's premier regional summer theaters, the Williamstown Theater Festival in Massachusetts. He appeared with both their mainstage and touring companies and worked with such actors, directors, and writers as Blythe Danner, Frank Langella, Joel Grey, Austin Pendleton, Steve Lawson, and Arthur Miller. During the next twelve years, Mr. Keller lived in Los Angeles, but continued working in both LA and New York, starring in over twenty five regional and off-Broadway productions. In addition to guest star and recurring roles in over twelve episodics and sitcoms, he expanded his involvement in the industry when he produced four plays in three years in Los Angeles, garnering him ten awards and nominations from Los Angeles drama critics.

During this same period, Mr. Keller regularly attended a professional acting class taught by his mentor, Milton Katselas. This relationship provided him with the opportunity to teach acting as well as pursue his love of acting. He then directed a number of plays, one of which received a special invitation from the French Theater Festival. Shortly thereafter, he was offered a position as a feature film story editor for a company on the Warner Bros. Lot. Mr. Keller went on to work in development for Atlas Entertainment, which produced such films as *Twelve Monkeys and Fallen.*

He became Director of Development at Cinergi Pictures, which produced the *Die Hard Trilogy* and *Evita*. After reading nearly twenty five hundred scripts and coverage's in three and a half years, Mr. Keller left development and is now a casting director for film, television and theatre.

0-595-29793-5

Printed in the United States
28637LVS00003BA/214-222

9 780595 297931